Be the Light

A Devotional

It's time to be reminded of the light He put inside of you. The light you are called to shine.

Annie Mayfield

Happy Self Publishing

Table of Contents

First and foremost, this is for Him.
The One who has never failed me yet.
Thank you to every person that has never
given up on me.

Especially Gwen, McRae, Lizzie, James, Mom, and Dad.
You are the brightest lights in my life.
Forever and always.

Hey you.

I just wanted to take a second and tell you that I am proud of you. Do you know how incredible you are? Do you realize everything you have gone through, survived, endured, and you're still here to tell the tale?

You're here, reading this work. You are taking a second to pour truth into your heart, mind, soul, and spirit, and that is something to be proud of. Life is hard, and it throws unexpected twists. I started this devotional at the beginning of the 2020 quarantine, thinking that by the time it was finished, I would be out. I am still in it. Not only that, but hardships have come up that I never in a million years would've expected to challenge my life in the way that they have, but hey, that's life, right? Things get hard, seasons grow dreary, and sometimes, it feels like the only thing you can possibly do to keep going is to focus on putting one foot in front of the other. Some days, it's hard to get out of bed, some evenings, it's hard to go to sleep, and sometimes, you have a pit of fear so large in your stomach that you actually feel ill. Then there are days you feel unstoppable, amazing, and as if the world is throwing absolutely everything it can in your favor your way. I just want to say I am proud of you. In all those seasons, I hope you remember Whose strength you have to rely on. He's never leaving you. No matter how alone you may feel, God's still got you. I hope that in our journey together these next 100 days, you discover that light that has always been, and always will be, inside of you. The light that makes you one of a kind. The light that allows you to mark this world in a way no one can. The light He put in you, to shine.

Your friend,

Annie

Know Who Defines You

> "God blesses you when people mock you and persecute
> you and lie about you and say all sorts of evil things
> against you because you are my followers. Be happy
> about it! Be very glad! For a great reward awaits you
> in heaven. And remember, the ancient prophets were
> persecuted in the same way."
> - Matthew 5:11-12

It is so easy for us to crawl into the pulpit of defining ourselves by others' opinions. Being a recovering people pleaser myself, I know just how easy it is to never want to speak your mind, truth, and what is on your heart for fear of what others' will say about you or how they will judge you for it. What is so important to know is that if you do speak your truth and live the purpose God has placed on your life, there is no question some people will talk about you. The truth is they were going to talk about you whether you live your God-ordained truth or not, so why not let the thing they are talking about at least be the same thing that makes you happy and feel fulfilled?

No one gets to control your life but yourself. No one gets to tell you how to act, who to be, what to say, or how to show up. People will talk about you, and when they do, remember that people talked down about Jesus too! Literally, the Savior of our world was so poorly talked about that it led to His death on the cross, how's that for fear of what others think about you? However, Jesus knew that the things He was saying and doing were in God's plan for Him, so He kept going. Do not let the hatred of others stop you from doing God's work in your life. The purpose God has placed on your life is far more important than other people's opinions. Keep going. Keep showing up. Follow that purpose, not the voice of what other people have to say about it.

God, I pray that today you help me live into the purpose you have placed on my life. I pray you make the voice of this purpose in my heart louder than the voice in my head that is influenced by other people's opinions that tell me I am not good, strong enough, smart enough, or capable enough. I am capable because You, within me, is capable. Help me to make Your voice in my heart the only voice I listen to.
Amen.

Shine Your Light

> "You are the light of the world- like a city on a hilltop
> that cannot be hidden."
> -Matthew 5:14

I think some of us are afraid of being seen as we truly are. That's why we like to text instead of call, put filters on our photos before we post them, and portray ourselves to the public in a way that doesn't tell the whole story of who we really are. When you prevent the world from seeing your true self, you are preventing them from seeing God's truth within you. You are filled with God's light; did you know that? He created you and deemed you "beautiful." When you try to be someone else or hide behind a status, rank, achievement, performance, or anything that can hide who you really are, you not only miss out on the miracle God created you to be for yourself, but you stop the world from seeing it too.

God put His love within us so it could shine it in the

unique way that only we can let it. If you spend your entire life looking at other people for how to act, live, speak, dress, and love, you will never experience how God intended for you to do all of those things. If you are truly living the life that He calls and wants you to live, you are letting the light He put inside of you shine- no matter how different it may look from everyone else's. Own your light. Shine your light. Never apologize for the light that is you. Always remember that those who you were made to live life with will only make your light shine brighter. Those that ask you to dim your light were never meant to be in your life.

God, I pray that in this very moment, you remind me of the special gifts you gave to me. You made me different from every single other person in this world for a reason. You made me unique and beautiful. You put this light inside of me for a reason, a reason that glorifies you. I pray you give me the strength to shine it. Every day All day and not apologize for it.
Amen

Remember Your Strength

> "God blesses you when people mock you and persecute
> you and lie about you and say all sorts of evil things
> against you because you are my followers. Be happy
> about it! Be very glad! For a great reward awaits you
> in heaven. And remember, the ancient prophets were
> persecuted in the same way."
> - Matthew 5:11-12

Do you ever get the feeling that you are not enough? That you aren't capable enough or strong enough to get the thing done that you are striving for? I feel this way a lot. In my heart, I can feel all of the things God has put here for me to dream of accomplishing, yet in my head, I have this voice of doubt that always tells me I am not good enough. It says I'm not smart enough. Not pretty enough. Not "fit" enough. Not a good enough speaker. Not bold enough. Not loud enough. Not rich enough. There is always this feeling of "not enough" in my stomach that makes me question if I can actually do the things I know God has called me to do.

Let me remind you of the thing I must remind myself of in times where I don't feel strong enough. It isn't your own strength that you must rely on to get you through your battles, but the Lord's. The Lord would not have entrusted you with a purpose that He Himself was not ready to carry out through you. I think, so many times, we put ourselves in this mindset of lonesomeness. We think it is us against the world, and because of that, we begin to feel weak. It isn't you against the world, because the God that created the entire world is on your side. He is for you. He is working for your good and your success. Remind yourself the next time you don't feel enough for something; it is God's love that makes you enough, and His strength in you that will carry you through. Stop relying fully on yourself, and start relying fully on God.

Lord, I pray right now, that you help me open my heart to receive your strength in its entirety. No more can I stand here and act like I have it all figured out when I have no idea what I am doing. I need you. I need your strength. I need you to act through me to fulfill this purpose you have placed in my heart.
Amen.

Trust God's Timing

> "For the revelation awaits an appointed time; it speaks of the end and will not prove false. Though it lingers, wait for it; it will certainly come and will not delay" Habakkuk 2:3

Do you ever get frustrated because you think your life should be happening a certain way, and it just isn't there yet? That maybe you aren't where you thought you'd be right now? Perhaps you are in a place in your life where you thought you'd be married right now, with children right now, having gotten your college degree right now, be on stage speaking to millions right now, literally, in a place so far from where you are. The reality of faith? It all comes down to believing that God's timing is better than our own. If God truly desires for certain things to happen in our life, they will happen. Just because it hasn't happened yet, does not mean they never will. Even Jesus wasn't called to start His ministry until He was 30. I am sure at 25 years old or 26, there was some part of Him that felt ready to go, but the Lord said not yet. Right now? I thought I'd know where I'd be employed after I graduated college. I thought I would've been a professional speaker talking to churches and large groups of people at self-development conferences. I thought I would've hit the New York Times bestsellers list. Not only has that not happened, but I feel so far from that happening. I am sure you can relate to some degree.

Remember this, my friend, God is never late. He is never wrong. He is never early either. He knows exactly what He is doing, why He is doing it, and when He is doing it. The hardest part about that? It is trusting it when we cannot see it right now. Trust that His timing is for you and your success even if it doesn't align with the timeline you initially had in place for yourself. Just keep showing up and remembering that He's got you, and when the time is right, everything He wants for you will come into fruition.

God, I pray that today, you remind me of your timing. It is good. It is true. It is for your glory I wish you to give me the strength to believe in the timing you have for my life and my endeavors, in that they always glorify you in exactly the way you need them to. Amen.

Above All Else, Be Kind

> *"Do not let kindness and truth leave you. Bind them around your neck, write them on the tablet of your heart"* Proverbs 3:3

Sometimes it's hard to know exactly who I am supposed to be. Do you ever feel that way? I feel that, every day, there are messages coming in from all directions on how I am supposed to be, look, dress, speak, and act. As a woman, society tells me to be feminine but not too feminine because that could be taken as weak. It tells me to be strong but not bossy. To be bold but not off-putting. To be independent but not headstrong. To be pretty but not "asking for it." To speak my mind, but only if it aligns with the things other people are saying.

There are so many different messages on who to be, how to act, all the things. Sometimes I don't even know who I actually want to show up as because I am hearing all these signals from so many different places on how I should be at that moment. In these moments, I remind myself that kindness looks good on everyone. The only thing that I truly always need to be is kind. I need to be kind to the people around me and myself. I can be whoever I want to be, as long as that identity is clothed in kindness always.

God, I pray you remind me that the only thing I absolutely must be every single day is kind. Kindness and love are the only things that need to be constant in my life because that is how you have called me to live.
Amen.

Be an Expert on Your Pain

> *"The Lord is close to the brokenhearted and saves those who are crushed in spirit"* Psalm 34:18

Earlier today, I looked at a video done by an astronaut talking about how he survived self-isolation in space for five months straight. Can you imagine? Five months of no one to talk to, hug, cry to, lean on, physically touch, or even look at? This man talked about how to accomplish what he set out to do in space, he needed to be aware of what he was risking. He needed to be an expert on his pain. Whenever he got scared, he reminded himself that fear is not the same thing as danger. Whatever he was afraid of at that moment did not necessarily mean he was in danger at that moment. He needed to go to that feeling of fear and figure out exactly what it was that stirred that inside of him, to sort through it and become stronger because of it.

What fear in your life are you resisting dealing with because you are associating it with danger? What pains in your life right now are stopping you from dealing with the situation and emotions upfront, in order to overcome them? That's the truth, my friends, you've got to be able to go to that place where your pain lies in order to move past it. God is close to the brokenhearted. God is right there with you as you navigate your way through the pain. The best part? Your pain serves a purpose in our Heavenly Father's eyes, even if that purpose is to simply downgrade your ego so your heart can be introduced to spiritual healing. A wound cannot heal unless it is revealed. Reveal your wounds. Let your Father heal them. Go to your pain point with the intention of owning up to them to your Savior, so that He can heal you from within.

God, in this moment, I show you to my wounds. I reveal all the pains in my heart to you. Do something with them. Heal me. Through the healing of me, use this as leverage to help heal others.
Amen.

You are Rare

> "Do not be conformed to this world, but be transformed by the renewal of your mind, that by testing you may discern what is the will of God, what is good and acceptable and perfect." Romans 12:2 "Do not be conformed to this world, but be transformed by the renewal of your mind, that by testing you may discern what is the will of God, what is good and acceptable and perfect." Romans 12:2

We live in a world right now where it is easier than ever to compare yourself. You fall into that scroll-hole on Instagram, Twitter, Facebook, Snapchat, and now TikTok, and all you can think is how much better everyone else's life seems to be than yours. "That girl wears the bathing suit so much better than me," "that guy seems to be so much happier than me," "they were invited to that party, and I wasn't." "I could never be as successful as them or make as much money as she does." We do it to ourselves every day, probably without even realizing it. The problem with this is that when we spend all of our energy toward looking at what we aren't and what we don't have, we take energy away from our ability to focus on the gifts God did give us. We are all uniquely and beautifully made for a specific reason that aligns with God's intentions for us. Everyone has different gifts, talents, and blessings, and if you spend your entire life looking at someone else, you are going to miss out on the miracle God created you to be. Stop looking to this world for an indication of how to act, who to be, when to speak, and what to dream. If you let others determine how you live your life, you'll live a life that supports their version of happiness, not yours. God made you special, unique, and rare for a reason. Stop getting stuck in comparing your life to everyone else's and own up to the one of a kind masterpiece that is your life in progress. Your differences are the gifts God gave you to mark this world in a way that no one else can, to fulfill a purpose He has for your life.

Stop looking down at your screen for the answers to how well you're doing at life and start looking up to God to pinpoint you in the direction He knows you need to go toward to find everlasting fulfillment and satisfaction in this life.

Lord, I take this second just to say thank you. Thank you for making me one of a kind. I am so sorry that up until this point I haven't honored that in the way I should. I pray you give me the strength to not only accept my differences but see them as gifts that you have given me to bless this world with.
Amen.

Your Calling

> *"To this you were called, because Christ suffered for you, leaving you an example, that you should follow in his steps." Peter 2:21*

ere's a statement that shocks absolutely no one- life gets busy. Whatever age you are at, you have an enormous number of things to do. One day you're in high school, and you have glee club, classes, basketball, student government, and social life, then you turn 40, and you have a job, taxes, bills, kids, and a marriage to maintain. Thing is, even though our lives are busy on paper, more than ever, people are left with this feeling of unfulfillment and dissatisfaction in their life. Pastor Ben Stuart put it the best way when he said people are like octopuses on rollerblades-there's a lot of movement going on but not a lot of progress. I want you to remember that your busy work is not your life's work. When God sent His son to die for us, it wasn't so you could go about your day working your 9-5 and attending geometry class. Not to say those things are not important, but let us not confuse them for our life's work. Our life's work is to serve and love each other in the way Jesus loved us. That is what we are called to do. I believe true happiness occurs when your heart of passion meets your heart of service. Every single one of our purposes in life is the same- to love on another, and in doing so, serve our God. How we do that looks different for everyone. A lawyer serves society in a different way than a surgeon, both are beautiful and align with the purpose God made them to have, but both are very different from one another.

I want to remind you to bring your life's work into your busy work. Yes, I know you may not necessarily enjoy your job to the fullest, or your classes, but that occupation does not define your calling. Your calling is to serve others. You were given that calling by your Father when He sent His son to die for you. Show up every day to your busy work with the intention of leaving it with your life's work. How many people can you love today? How can you make sure you are showing up as your best self today to serve the people you are there to serve? Your life's calling- serve other people using God's example.

God, remind me of my life's work. I want my everyday actions to resemble the calling you placed on my life the minute you gave your son up for ransom to pay the debt of my sins. Give me the strength to serve others the way you served me to fulfill my life's calling.
Amen.

Keep Going

<blockquote>
"Let us not become weary in doing good, for at the proper time we will reap a harvest if we do not give up." Galatians 6:9
</blockquote>

Do you ever hit that point in your day where you're just exhausted? You feel like you have given that day absolutely everything you have to give, yet it still feels like you haven't even made a dent in your to-do list. What about in life? You ever feel like you keep going and going and going, yet there seems to be no progress whatsoever to show for it?

I've been there before. I have had dreams where, day in and day out, I have put in massive tons of work toward those dreams, and yet, at the end of every single day, from the surface, it looks as if I did nothing. That is the beauty of a dream, though. I think we forget to look underneath the surface when it comes to checking for progress. When plants grow, the first thing to grow is the root, not the bud. This is because the root is the strongest and sturdiest part of the crop, and without a strong root, you will not have a strong harvest. That is the same thing with our dreams. God puts dreams in our heart, and when we decide to go for them, in the forefront of the journey toward the accomplishment of that dream, it may seem like nothing is happening. It may look as if your business isn't growing at all, that relationship isn't going anywhere, your music career isn't making any progress, yet the reality of it is throughout the entire time you think nothing is happening because of the lack of results at the surface, your roots are growing underneath. The problem is that most people quit before the bud even gets a chance to grow and give the people a harvest. Don't be one of those people. Keep going. Keep growing. Keep doing the work you need to do because your roots are growing, even if you can't see them. One day, you will reap the harvest of all of your good work, but you must still be around to see it.

Lord, I pray you give me the strength to keep going. I want to see the day all of my hard work grows up into a harvest. Give me the endurance to make to that point, and to never give up on myself or the dreams you gave me.
Amen.

Grown-up Gratitude

> *"Be joyful always, pray continually, give thanks in all circumstances for this is God's will for you in Christ Jesus." Thessalonians 5:16-8*

Sometimes I think we give thanks to God in a way that makes us seem like children. When we pray, we say thank you for my house, my family, my money, my health, and basically, all the things that we can see. There is nothing wrong with that, at all, but as Christians, I think we are called to a deeper gratitude than that which touches the surface of what God does for us. Mature gratitude doesn't just say thank you for His provisions, but for His presence.

What are you grounding your gratitude in? If it is in the things that you can only see, such as your job, bank account, savings, health, clothes, shelter, relationships, or whatever else lies on the surface in your life, then that is how deep your relationship with God will go- surface level. I want you to have a deep appreciation for God, one that goes beneath surface-level things. Remember to say thank you for the things in your life that God has given you that you don't even know about yet. Say thank you for the things you cannot see. Give thanks for the times God saved you, and you didn't even know about it. Rejoice in gratitude for the good you know is going to come your way even if you are in a dark storm right now, simply because you know who your Father is. When you start to become grateful for God's presence instead of His provisions, your life will change. The constant cycle of good and bad times won't happen anymore. Why? Because His presence never goes away. That is the only constant in our lives. Your shoes, clothes, house, money, relationships...they all may change, but His presence in your life won't. Now that is truly something to be grateful for.

My God, remind me of your true gift today, the gift of your presence. Bring me back into the realization that your love is all that I need to be sustained. All the surface-level, materialistic things should not be the source of my gratitude, your presence should. Help me walk in that.
Amen.

Set Your Standards High

> "Do not be misled: bad company corrupts good character." Corinthians 15:33

Did you know that you are an accumulation of the top 5 people you spend the most time with? I don't just mean your top 5 streaks on Snapchat, I mean the top 5 people you talk to, listen to, hang around, and spend time with the most. The first time I heard that, I was a freshman in college, and that very statement terrified me. Not because I didn't believe it, but the opposite- because I did. At the time, I had some "friends" that I surrounded myself with in my life that I didn't necessarily want to be like. They were making choices about drugs, sex, and alcohol that my heart didn't feel inclined to do. That being said, had I not distanced myself after realizing that no matter how strong you are in your ways and beliefs, the more time you spend around people, the more you are influenced by them, I get nauseous even thinking about where or who I could be right now.

Whether you realize it or not, who you hang out with has an extraordinary impact on your life. I bet you that you weren't much of a cusser until your friends started cussing, and then, you slowly but surely started letting them slip like a sailor. I guarantee that if every single one of your girlfriends started numbing the pain of their own dysfunction by gossiping about everyone else's, you would start to do the same. Whether you like it or not, your friends have an enormous influence over you. That is why it is so important to have high standards for who we choose to spend our time with. I am not saying be a jerk to anyone you don't agree with, because we are called to love all people. What I am saying is for the select few people that you allow into your heart, make sure they are people who inspire you, and make you a better person. When you look at how these people are living their lives, are they living in a way that you would be proud to live your life too? If the answer to that is yes, then you have a top-notch friend for life. If it is no, maybe it's time to loosen the reins on that friendship a bit, not completely, but do not let that person have the chance to influence you into behaving like them.

God, you have given me such an incredible life. I pray that you help me discern in this moment the friendships that truly grow me, build me up, and help strengthen my relationship with you.
Amen.

You are Enough

> *But he said to me, "My grace is sufficient for you, for my power is made perfect in weakness." Therefore, I will boast all the more gladly about my weaknesses, so that Christ's power may rest on me. That is why, for Christ's sake, I delight in weaknesses, in insults, in hardships, in persecutions, in difficulties. For when I am weak, then I am strong. - 2 Corinthians 12:9-10*

Have you ever felt you're not good enough? Like you're going and going, trying and trying, yet it doesn't seem like you're getting anywhere? I feel like that a lot. I sometimes get overwhelmed with feelings of confusion, uncertainty, and doubt. Just today, in the car, I got emotional and asked God, "what is it exactly that you want from me?" Sometimes, it feels like I am not good enough, smart enough, strong enough, or capable enough to do the things that I know God has called me to do. I think that's the point of God's grace, though. It is the moment that we do not feel good enough on our own, or strong enough, or capable enough that we open ourselves up to surrendering to God's strength. If we feel completely certain and strong enough on our own, we wouldn't need God. That is why, whenever you are striving for something that you don't feel good enough to accomplish, I truly believe that is the greatest indication you are on the right path. God wants you to rely on Him. Every weakness, insult, hardship, persecution, and difficulty (yes, I just reiterated the verse from above), He wants you to realize that you are not enough on your own to get through it, but His strength in you makes you strong enough. His intelligence in you makes you smart enough. His capabilities in you make you capable enough. The moment you realize it isn't your strength you can rely on, but His, you are allowing so much more to be done with your life through Him than could ever be done through just you alone. Accept the hardships, embrace the unknowns, keep going and keep trying, not because you aren't going to fail or fall, but because His strength in you will always pick you back up on the path He chose for you to walk on this earth. You are enough because He makes you enough.

God, give me the strength to realize it isn't my capabilities I need to rely on, but Yours within me. You turn all bad into good, so every failure of mine is really just another chance for me to experience your grace.
Amen.

Let Yourself Be Seen

> "For am I now seeking the approval of man, or of God?
> Or am I trying to please man? If I were still trying
> to please man, I would not be a servant of Christ."
> *Galatians 1:10*

There's that point in our lives where we have a decision to make. We can choose to step into the person God created us to be or be molded into the version of the ideal that society wants us to become. When I say "version of the ideal" I mean a person that has the looks, the car, the attractive spouse, the clothes, the newest iPhone, the blue check by their Instagram handle- basically, anything outside of them that makes them seem that they have life all figured out. It is so easy to want those things too. It's easy to want to appear to have it all figured out on the outside, and completely neglect to want to work out the hardship we feel on the inside. The problem with that, though, is that who you truly are as a person lies on the inside of you, not the outside. How do I know that? Because that is where God lies in each and every one of us- on the inside. God made us in His image, and think about it, when you build something, you cannot build it from the outside in, you must always build from the inside out. It's just the basic law of construction. You must start on the inside before you begin decorating the outside. That's how I see everything that is on the outside of us- as decorations. It isn't who we truly are, but simply part of what we are. You can have a Christmas tree without the ornaments, but you cannot have a Christmas tree without the tree. Think about that.

Let yourself be seen for what is inside of you, not your decorations. Your decorations or your hair, clothes, car, job, jewelry, and shoes may help express who you are, but they are not the means to define who you are. Let the world see the real you that lies underneath. The one that resembles our God and the part of you He built in His image when He started His works within you.

Lord, open me up to this world. Give me the strength to be seen without all the things that I try to hide behind. Help me embrace the part of me that resembles You and be brave enough to let the entire world see.
Amen.

Who Are You Trying to Please?

> *"For am I now seeing the approval of man, or of God? Or am I trying to please man? If I were still trying to please man, I would not be a servant of Christ."*
> *Galatians 1:10*

One of my favorite girl crushes of all time is none other than the magnificent, incredible, amazing, motivational keynote speaker and author Rachel Hollis. One of the reasons I love her so much is that I resonate with her. She, like myself, is what I like to call a "recovering people pleaser." I did not coin that term, that credit belongs to Rachel, but I relate to it so much because, for my entire life, I have tormented myself over making other people happy. When I say torment myself, I don't want you thinking it is a bad thing to make other people happy, it absolutely is not, but making others happy should be more of a side effect to whatever you choose to do rather than the main goal itself. You see, it isn't truly possible to make someone else happy, that is entirely on them to do. You are not responsible for someone else's happiness. This was a lesson that took me forever to learn, and because of that, I experienced much anxiety in my life.

Rachel says that whenever you are feeling anxious, ask yourself, "who am I trying to please?" and then ask yourself, "who am I having to be in order to please that person?" We get anxious when there is a disconnect between the person we know we truly are, and the person we are showing up as to (more often than not) please someone else. What if we dedicated every single moment of our lives not living to please other people, but to please our Heavenly Father? To strive every day to honor His glory and excellence with the way we act, speak, give, move, and love? I guarantee you that the minute you start showing up every day to please Him instead of everyone else, whatever anxieties are weighing you down will lighten their load. You will become a more authentic version of yourself when you show up as someone that resembles, He who created you.

My Heavenly Father, hear me today as I cry out to you with all this weight of anxiety and desire to gain approval from everyone else around me. You are the only One I need approval from. Help me see that and walk in your light, for your light only
Amen.

God Will Still Be There

> "About the ninth hour Jesus cried out with a loud voice saying, 'My God, My God, why have you forsaken me?" Matthew 27:46

When I was little, and something was upsetting me, I was never afraid to yell at my family in a desperate attempt to alleviate some of the agitation inside of me. Was it right? Absolutely not, but I am blessed enough to say that I knew my family wasn't going anywhere, even after they saw the worst side of me. Now, I'll be honest; I would never yell at my friends the way I have yelled at my family before. I could never show my friends that "Godzilla" side of me, because I didn't know if they would ever talk to me again. My family, though? I knew no matter how much I screamed, shouted, or exploded, they would still be there the next day, loving me just the same.

Here's the thing. I think people are afraid to truly express what they are feeling to God. When we are upset, angry, sad, fearful, agitated, and seriously just mad, we are too afraid to express to God what is causing us so much pain. Have you ever just absolutely let it all out to God? I don't mean a put-together, movie kind of let-it-all-out but a full-on eyes are swollen, hair looks like it has never seen a hairbrush, veins popping out of your neck kind of let-it-all-out. I think we treat our relationship with God with the same reservations that hold us back from showing our friends or strangers on the street the true side of us. It's almost as if we're afraid that by showing Him how upset we are, He's not going to be there for us tomorrow.

Let me reassure you that God can handle whatever emotions you throw at Him. You feel sad? Show it. You feel hurt? Express it. You're angry as hell? Let it out, my friend! God wants you to take Him to that place. He wants you to treat Him like those people that you know no matter what, they will still be there tomorrow.

Even Jesus cast out His questions and emotions to God. You are invited into that same relationship.

God, remind me of your never-ending presence. You will always be there for me. I pray for the reminder that you want me to show you my pain and weaknesses. You crave to see what is heavy on my heart and ask for me to cast it to you.
Amen.

Rejection is Redirection

> *"As you come to Him, as a living stone rejected by men but in the sight of God chosen and precious."* 1 Peter 2:4

Getting rejected sucks. I do not think there is one person on this earth that would say being rejected by other people is necessarily a *good* feeling that they crave more of. In fact, I would argue that the majority of people do whatever they can in their power to prevent rejection from happening in their lives. As humans, we mold ourselves into this societal ideal in the hope that we will prevent anyone from rejecting us in the process. That's why most people fail to ever accomplish the dreams that God put in their hearts because they are too afraid of what others will say about them as they try to pursue them.

Les Brown, a top motivational speaker, says all the time that the most expensive piece of property on this earth is the graveyard. The reason being that more priceless ideas, dreams, inventions, innovations, and hopes die there alongside the people because those people were afraid to act on them in their lifetime.

Here's how I view rejection. I think that if someone or something was meant to be in your life, it would be. That being said, if someone rejects you from a job offer, a friendship, a relationship, or anything that you ever so desire, it really is God just taking you in a different direction. A direction that will, in return, take you toward the destination He needs you to go in, and if that person or thing did not reject you, to begin with, you would never have followed the path God needed you to go down. Be thankful for rejection; it is really just redirection in disguise.

God, thank you for every single rejection in my life that has gotten me to this point. Thank you in advance for all the rejections to come that will take me toward the place you need me to go to fulfill your purpose in me.
Amen.

Get Up the Hill

> *"Consider it pure joy, my brothers and sisters, whenever you face trials of many kinds, because you know that the testing of your faith produces perseverance." James 1:2-3*

There is a saying in the running community that how you take the hill is how you take life. In a run, people take on a large hill in different ways. Some people slow down because they want to conserve energy for the hill, some people speed up to get over the hill as quickly as possible, and some people see the hill and turn around, so they do not have to face the pain of struggling up it. Which one are you? I don't necessarily mean in regard to running, even though that is a great thing to identify as well, but in life. When adversity or struggle comes your way, do you slow down, speed up to charge it head-on, or turn away from it?

Here's the thing. It's not so much about how you get up the hills you are going to face in life, as it is getting up the hill itself. It doesn't have to look pretty, be smooth, or necessarily make you feel like superman or woman, it just has to be something that you get up and over. I have come to learn it is an honor to experience struggle, pain, hardship, and obstacles. It is an honor to have a "hill" arise in your life that you are barely able to get up. The adversity and obstacles we face are what builds up our faith muscles. Just like how exercise strengthens your physical muscles, adversity in life strengthens our spiritual muscles. God will put you in a storm to remind you who is bigger than the storm. He will allow for there to be a challenge in your life if, in return, it means you grow in your faith and deepen your connection with Him.

Whatever "hill" you are trying to get up in your life right now, remember that His strength will get you up that hill, all you have to do is keep going and not run away from it. In the end, you will be stronger because of that hill.

God, I want to take a second to say thank you for my hills. Thank you for the struggles I have been through, am currently in, and am going to go through because they remind me who's strength I can truly depend on. Amen.

Remember What Unconditional Love Means

> *"There is no fear in love. But perfect love drives out fear, because fear has to do with punishment. The one who fears is not made perfect in love." 1 John 4:18*

There was a quote I saw on Instagram this morning that had me jump up and down around my kitchen, I loved it so much. It read, "God isn't mad at you because you didn't read your Bible or pray. When you understand His love for you isn't dependent on what you do, you'll want to read your Bible and pray." Now I can't give credit where credit is due because I have absolutely no idea who wrote this, but if, in fact, you are reading this right now and you wrote it, you hit the nail on the head.

I think so many people cannot possibly wrap their heads around what unconditional love means. This is shown by the way people continue to think when they mess up, God is mad at them, or for some weird turn of events, God's love for us depends on the amount of our Bible annotations and how many times we go to church on Sunday. This couldn't be further from the truth. Nothing you can do could ever deserve God's love. I don't care what your record looks like, church attendance is, or even how much you donate to the church at Christmas time. God loves you because you are His child, enough said there's nothing else to it. What I get so upset about is I think people are so confused by that concept, because in our society, we are ingrained to think that you have to "earn" whatever you get, including love and affection, and in that confusion, when people do mess up, they run away from God instead of running toward Him. This is because they think, for some reason, He is "mad" at them, and they wish to suppress this fear instead of owning up to it with God. Let me take some pressure off you real fast; there is no fear in the love God has for us. Read the verse above. God's love for us is *perfect*, a love that we humans are incapable of giving but are blessed enough by His grace to receive. Whatever mistakes you've made or didn't make, things you said or didn't say, places you went or didn't go, people you hurt or didn't hurt, God doesn't base His love for you on that. He bases it on the fact you are His child, and He created you in His image. *That* is the invitation you and I are invited to accept through His unconditional love.

God, remind me what your love means. Remind me of its perfection and give me the humility to realize that I did nothing to deserve it. I could not earn your perfect love, yet you gave it to me anyway. Help me live my life in a way that glorifies that.
Amen.

Stay Humble

> "The Lord almighty has a day in store for all the proud and lofty, for all that is exalted (and they will be humbled)." Isaiah 2:12

I was at a nutritional conference one time, and that Sunday morning, at the service, someone said something that has stuck with me ever since. Ego stands for edging God out. I think people have ego all wrong. In our minds, egotistical people are cocky, full of themselves, and walk around like they own the place. While, yes, that is a form of ego, I want to remind you that is simply one way ego can be portrayed. Ego is also thinking you are below people. When you walk into a room with people that make more money than you, in your mind, are prettier than you or are in better shape than you, and you label yourself as less value because of these factors, you are living by your ego. You are saying that we are not all equal in the eyes of God, we are not all children of God, regardless of salary or fitness caliber. That is edging God out.

Remember that God loves us all the same. No matter what clothes we wear, how much money we make, the country clubs we are a part of or the guy we are dating. All these things mean nothing to God; what matters to Him is our hearts. Every day, I say to myself in the mirror, "today I have no ego. I am neither above nor below anyone." I don't care if it's Bill Gates or the homeless person living down the street. You are not more or less valuable than any single person when you look at yourself and others through the lens of your Heavenly Father, who loves us all the same.

Lord, I pray you give me the clarity to see through your lens today. I am neither above nor below anyone. We are all children of yours, and I pray you give me the strength to choose to not live from my ego, but your grace.
Amen.

Yes, You Can

> "That the man of God may be competent, equipped for every good work." 2 Timothy 3:17

You ever feel not good enough for something you've got to do? I feel that way a lot. Sometimes I just get in my own head so much that even for little things I know I am capable of doing, I will psych myself out, and all of a sudden think that I can't. That's the thing about God, though, He uses the ordinary to do extraordinary things because of His strength. He calls you not because you are competent in your own capabilities, but in His.

When you embrace Him, you are embracing His strength to act through you. Whatever it is you have on your plate, yes, you can do that thing. Remember whose strength is acting through you. You have all the competence in the world because you can rely on His competence to act through you in whatever situation He has put you in. God wants us to embrace His strength and accept that we alone, are not enough to do what He needs us to do in this world, because it is in that surrender, we allow His capabilities to work through us.

Today, I want you to surrender. Live your life in that place of surrender. Even in the greatest of uncertainties, you can have certainty that your God has got it all figured out. He not only nurtures you but fortifies you for every battle He needs you to face to strengthen you. You can do this because your God in you can do this.

God, remind me that today I can. I can because you give me all the strength that I need to carry out whatever it is you have planned for my life. Yes, I can. I can because You can.
Amen.

You Are Not What Others Think of You

> *"It is dangerous to be concerned with what others think of you, but if you trust the Lord, you are safe."*
> *Proverbs 29:25*

My entire life, I have struggled with this fear of what other people think of me. It began just as a kid with my parents. I was so driven to make them proud, and because of that, I created this habit of incessantly wanting to please other people. Whatever I did, I did because I wanted to make other people like me and to please them. I am not diagnosing myself, but I am certain I had a phobia of making other people uncomfortable. I never wanted to make someone unhappy, sad, or put them in a position where they didn't like me. Where did this lead me, you may ask? Straight toward the depths of unhappiness. You see, in doing that, I was acting like someone that I wasn't. I wasn't doing the things that made me happy, simply because I was spending all my energy on doing things that other people wanted me to do to make them happy. I wasn't showing up as the person God created me to be.

That's the thing, you guys. A lot of times, God gifts us with these special and unique gifts that, unfortunately, the world scoffs at because they are "different." Anything different from the majority is ultimately labeled as wrong or bad, and I do think that letting go of what others think of you is the price to pay for living your God-ordained life. I have not yet reached the point where I am totally immune to other people's opinions, and I don't know if that point even exists. What I am certain of, though, is that the closer I get in my relationship to God, the volume of other people's opinions tends to decrease. You may not be capable of letting the fear in your heart of what others think of you completely go away, but you can quieten it with increasing God's voice in your heart.

God, I pray you help me release this pressure I put on myself to live up to what others think of me. I am yours, that is all I need in order to live the fulfilled life you planned for me to live.
Amen.

Your Pain Has a Purpose

What's in your heart right now? Fear? Rejection? Deceit? Bitterness? Pressure? Anxiety?

A lot of times, I wake up to these feelings haunting me. It's like I don't even need an alarm clock; my anxiety will just wake me up in the morning. There's always that blissful second right when you wake up where you don't remember everything that happened the day before or that is currently weighing heavy on your heart, but then, just as soon as that moment comes, it passes, and with its passing, the realization of all the things that you are upset about arrives.

When I feel really heavy in the heart, I always remember that God doesn't just accept pain, He uses it. Every single scratch, scar, broken, and cracked piece is used in His creation of who we are meant to be. Yes, I mean all of your mistakes. All of your wrongdoings. All of those bad habits. All of the bad choices and decisions, they all can be used by God to do wonderful works within you, as crazy as it seems. Even if that mighty work is simply the realization that in those moments you chose to distance yourself from the person God created you to be, He'll use that. He wants you to live the life He designed for you because He knows that is the way you will be the most fulfilled. In living that life, He also knows all the mistakes and poor choices you are going to make that distance you from the life He called you to live, yet His love for us goes so far that even those poor choices can be used for good. Just like the verse says, *all things work together for good.* Not just the times you are on your best behavior, but also the times when you aren't. God's going to use your pain for a purpose, always. He will always turn even the darkest of storms into the most beautiful of sunrises.

God, remind me today that you have a purpose for all of these things that rest heavily on my heart. All the bad, hard, challenging, and uncertain things that I cannot shake, please help me rest in knowing that You aren't just accepting of them, but You are going to use them for good.
Amen.

You Have All You Need

> "You already have all you need. You already have more access to God than you can handle."
> 1 Corinthians 4:8

Sometimes I think it's really easy to look around at everyone else's life and think we don't have all that we need to make something of our own. Throw in social media and the ability to instantly see how much better everyone else seems to be doing than us, and it is so easy to think that we aren't as strong, pretty, handsome, capable, smart, or responsible enough to do anything with our lives.

That's the thing, though, my beautiful friends, God gave you all that you need to live the life He planned for you to live. You may not be as funny as that person, smart as that other person, fit or strong as the guy you see on your Instagram feed, attractive as the girl who just got crowned Miss USA, but you were given exactly the characteristics that God needed you to have to fulfill His purpose for your life. You have all that you need, and more than that, you have Him. He gave you all the pieces to the puzzle that is your life that will be required to live the life He has planned for you. Next time you think you aren't enough or don't have enough to do what you want to do, look at it as an indication that maybe that isn't the direction God wants you to go in. You will always feel like you have the right pieces of the puzzle for whatever it is you want to do if you are truly walking in God's path for you because He gave you all that you need.

Stop looking around at what everyone else has and start looking inside yourself to evaluate all it is that you have that God is asking you to use to accomplish the task He set for you to accomplish on this earth.

God, I pray you help me shift my focus to all the things I do have rather than do not. I trust that you are for me, and because of that, I will always have what I need if I am living into the path you have set for me.
Amen.

One Mile at a Time

I came home from a 6hr drive yesterday to find a gift from my very best friend. It's a bracelet that says, "one mile at a time." If anyone knows me, they know I am insanely in love with running. I think it is the most amazing thing in the world to go for a nice 20 miler and get lost in my thoughts and the music. Most people are so confused when I say I love a good long run, but here's the secret I have found to running long distance- you cannot judge how mile 10 will be based on mile 1. Every single mile has to be its own checkmark. You cannot be looking forward to getting mile 15 over with if you're only on mile 4, you've got to take it one mile at a time.

What I realized over time is how much better my life seems to feel when I treat the mentality of living just like I do my mentality on a long run. So many times, I want to fix something that is lightyears away from the moment I am currently in, or my mind is so focused on the thing 10 activates down on my to-do list that I am not even focused on the activity I am currently doing. God wants us to live a life taking one thing at a time. Just like this bible verse says, His word is a lamp for our feet. The thing about a lamp, though? Its light only goes so far. God doesn't show us the full picture for a reason, He wants us to take our lives one day at a time. I hope you start living your life with the mentality of a long-distance runner, focusing on every step and every mile, fully grasping each moment it is giving you. The course is God's job, but your job is to stay obedient to the course and take your life one mile at a time.

God, today, I pray for the patience to stay the course. I don't need to have it all figured out, that's your job. I just need to walk in faith, one step at a time. Amen.

Calm the Inner Waves

> "He got up, rebuked the wind and said to the waves "Quiet, be still!" Then the wind died down and it was completely calm." Mark 4:39

I was listening to a sermon this morning all about anxiety by Steven Furtick. I don't know about you, but anxiety is something I struggle with every single day. I wake up before my alarm clock some days just because I am so incredibly anxious. My head starts racing, and my thoughts are going a million miles an hour, and I just can't seem to turn it off. The things I am anxious about span all the way from my body image and how I feel that it looks, to my job, to what the next topic for my next book is going to be about, to where the heck my dog is, to what my boyfriend is thinking, and can go to the depths of imagining a scenario going awry two years from this moment. That's the beauty of anxiety- it doesn't have a limit on the time frame it can get you caught up in. You can be anxious about something that's 2 minutes away or 20 years away.

Steven Furtick made a point in his sermon that was so profound. When Jesus calmed the storm with the disciples in the boat, He did it to teach them a lesson. Just as Jesus calmed the storm outside, we can calm the storm inside of us. As long as you keep Jesus and God in your heart, just as the disciples had Jesus in their boat, you can remain calm amidst the storm. Here's the thing friends- it isn't about the storm that's raging outside of you (your circumstances) that is causing you pain, it is the inner storm that no one gets to see. It's depression. The anxiety. The pressure. The inner critic. The guilt. The shame. The jealousy. Those are the waves in your heart that are causing the storm that you feel raging inside you. You've got to go to *that* place. You have got to shift your focus from the outer storm to what's raging on inside of you. Take God to *that* place. Once you go there with Him and surrender to Him, you can't be touched by the storms raging outside of you because your heart is still. Your heart is at peace. Your heart is calm. Your heart is a boat with Jesus in it in the midst of any storm that comes your way.

Lord, remind me of the strength you have given me today. Help me have the bravery to take you to that place. To stop blaming what I feel on what's outside of me and face the storm that is raging within.
Amen.

Unveil Your Truth

> "Guard, through the Holy Spirit who dwells in us, the treasure which has been entrusted to you."
> 2 Timothy 1:14

The other day, I was running, listening to Oprah, as I usually do, and something she said completely stopped me in the middle of my run. She said that most people spend their entire life trying to transform into someone, when the true path to discovering our greatest selves is not a path of transformation but a path of unveiling. Everything you need to live the life you desire to live if you want to live a life growing into the highest expression of yourself is already inside you. People will spend their entire lives trying to make external things fill them up on the inside. They go after money, fame, fortune, Instagram likes, relationships, houses, cars, clothes, you name it! The reality is that none of those things provide for us the inner peace and happiness that, deep down, we are truly craving. What we crave to fill us up is already inside us- that is connection. We crave to be deeply understood, heard, seen, and marked as valuable. That part of us that craves this deep connection is inside the same body that holds it. Our God provides us the richest and deepest connection we could possibly have. The Holy Spirit also lies in us.

I think so many people become exhausted simply because they are going after things that may make them happy in the short term, but not the long term. To reach true happiness and fulfillment isn't about getting or achieving anything outside of you, it is about uncovering what has also been inside you since the day you came into this world- the Holy Spirit inside you. Once you can connect to that place in your heart, all the things outside you cannot compare to the feeling you get when you are deep in that connection to the Spirit. Stop looking for things to fill you up from the outside, start looking inward and connect to the divine which is, and has always been, inside you.

God, help me uncover all the layers I have built around my truest and highest self- which is the place where the Holy Spirit rests in me. I pray you give me the strength to resist outside temptation to fill me up but allow me to see that the only lasting fulfillment that exists is that which comes from connecting to the source inside me.
Amen.

Today, I Love My Body

> *"For the Lord sees not as man sees man looks on the outward appearance, but the Lord looks on the heart."'*
> *1 Samuel 16:7*

My entire life, I've felt that I have struggled with loving my body. I don't like the way my belly button looks like a frowny face when I sit down; I feel so uncomfortable in photos when I am on my left side because I am convinced that arm is 10x the size of what a regular arm should be, and I really don't like how my thighs rub together when I run. To add to the fact that, every day, it seems I am surrounded by Instagram photos and ads of women that have flawless bodies even while running, an activity where us mere mortals experience the rolls of our tummies bouncing up and down. Not to say I am out of shape; I am currently in the best shape of my life. I run 60-70 miles a week, and to add to that, do HIIT workouts 5 days a week. Therein lies the problem, though, even with all the exercise, which I love to do, and eating healthy, I still feel uncomfortable and gross in my body at times. I know this goes without saying, but you are so much more than your body. What's hard is that this simple realization isn't something that sinks in one time, and you "naturally" believe it every day. At least, in my case, this is something I have to remind myself of every single day. There are days I get up and feel so confident in my physical appearance, and there are days that I feel as if I am disgusting and repulsive. That's the thing about "outward appearance" and things that the world promotes, like what is said in the verse, they are not constant. Outer beauty, makeup, jewelry, money, and body image are things that are always coming and going. The real fruit of who we are stays constant- which is our reflection of Him in us. Your body is simply a vehicle that transmits your beauty into this world, not the means to define your body. I hope you remind yourself of this every single day. Do I encourage you to be healthy? Absolutely! I want you to feel your absolute best and have the best energy you possibly could, but I want you striving to get healthy for the purposes of allowing your body to experience the greatest energy it possibly can, not to strive for a certain body "image." We are not an image; we are an energy. Our worth lies in the parts of us that cannot be shown on ads, Instagram photos, or magazines- it lies in our hearts. Your beauty lies within. Instead of looking at your stomach in the mirror today, look at your smile.

God, I pray that you remind me where my beauty truly lies. I am yours, divinely and perfectly made. Help me nourish this body you gave me as a vehicle to show the world my true beauty- which is my heart.
Amen.

Do It Anyways

"Let us not become weary in doing good, for at a proper time we will reap a harvest if we do not give up" Galatians 6:9

Martina McBride has a song called *Anyway*, and I am not kidding you I'm surprised my boom box didn't bust open when I was little from the non-stop loop that I had this song on. There is one line in particular that I absolutely love, and it always puts a little fire in my belly when I hear it- "You can spend your whole life building, something for nothing, one storm can come and blow it all away, build it anyway."

Sometimes you are not going to feel like doing it. You are going to feel insecure, have doubts, feel gross, not be in the mood, worry about what other people are thinking, but you have got to keep building that thing you know in your heart God is asking you to build anyway. You may say, Annie, that's the thing- I don't know what it is God wants me to build. I can tell you, right now, if you don't have that exact "thing" you know you were put on this earth to do, then the thing you need to be building right now is your relationship with Him. Get into the word. Get yourself in a prayer group or a bible study. Do what you need to do even if you don't necessarily feel like it, because anyone can do the thing they need to do when they are feeling like a million bucks and full of confidence, what counts is what you do when you don't feel like doing it. Do you still go to the gym? Read your bible? Work your business? Build that relationship? Write that letter? Say your prayers? *Especially* when you don't feel like it? It's when you don't feel like it, your true commitment to whatever it is you said you were going to do, shows.

God, help me do it anyway. I may not understand or even see the plan you have for my life right now but give me the discipline and strength to choose every day to move the needle of my life toward you in whatever ways I have control over right now.
Amen.

I Am Not What They Say

> "It is dangerous to be concerned with what others think of you, but if you trust the Lord, you are safe."
> Proverbs 29:25

I go through seasons of my life where I am absolutely unconcerned with what other people think of me. Then I have times where I feel like I am crippled by the fear of how everyone else is judging me. Let me be clear, when I say seasons, I mean days. Some days, I feel as if I am totally unstoppable, and I am only focusing on the fruitfulness of what the Lord has planned for me, other days, I am constantly searching for my validation in what other people think of me. Right now is one of those days where I am wondering, what do people think of me? Are they judging me? Do they think I am weird?

Here's the thing, my beautiful friends, you are always going to be in a place where people judge you. Whether you're doing something that makes you incredibly happy, or you do something that doesn't necessarily make you happy but you think makes other people happy, there are going to be people that judge you. Knowing that, why don't you just live the life that you enjoy living? The life that God laid all the pieces out in your heart for you to live.

Sometimes I get scared to show people my true self. I am afraid they think what I do is weird, how loud I am is annoying, how I dress is way too casual (athleisure for days), or I am overly vulnerable with the personal things I write about in my books. Thing is, I know deep down in my heart, I was called to be exactly who I am. I was called to have a loud voice, put emphasis on my fitness, so I basically live in athletic clothes, and speak to people's hearts through writings of my pain and struggles. Do some people judge it? Absolutely. Thing is, though, if I decided not to do those things simply out of the fear of other people judging me, I would still have people judging me for something else. You are not what other people say you are. You are what God says you are, which is His child. That is your truth, live in that every single day. If you do, you can sit at a table with other people's opinions and judgments all around you, and still be able to only focus on Him.

God, I pray you give me the strength today that I need to be the best version of myself. The version of myself that was made in your image and exudes all of the unique, magnificent gifts you gave me. Remind me that I am yours, and I am what you say I am.
Amen.

Use Your Gifts

> "God has given each of you a gift from His great variety of spiritual gifts. Use them well to serve one another" 1 Peter 4:10-11

We all have things within us that make us different from one another. This is something that when I was younger, I hated. I hated the fact that I had things about me that made me different from the crowd. Whether it was physical, like the birthmark that stretches about all of my lower right thigh, or internal like how I seem to be so much more expressive and emotional than a lot of the people I am surrounded by, I never liked the things that made me different.

What I've come to learn and embrace is that God gave us our differences so that we could use them to mark this world in a way that no one else can. There is only one wrong way to live your life, and that is to ignore all the gifts God gave you, no matter how different they may make you seem from the majority of people. Whether it be your gift to teach, swim, play basketball, cook, write, speak, or debate, God gave you your gift for a reason.

I believe that true bliss occurs when our heart of passion meets our heart of purpose. We are all called to the same purpose in this world, and that is to serve one another, just as it is said in the bible verse above. However, *how* we serve one another depends on the unique gifts that God has given us. Some are called to serve others through being a teacher, other lawyers, some people are supposed to be doctors, while some are meant to be actors and actresses. When we align this purpose of ours, to serve one another in this world, with the special gifts God has placed on our hearts, that is where ultimate fulfillment arises.

God, thank you for my gifts, no matter how different I may feel at times. I pray you give me the courage to use the gifts inside of me to walk into my purpose of serving others in this world.
Amen.

Do It Scared

> *"For I know the plans I have for you declares the Lord,*
> *plans for welfare and not for evil, to give you a future*
> *and a hope." Jeremiah 29:11*

This is probably my favorite bible verse of all time. I think I love it so much because it brings me so much comfort in situations where I am most uncomfortable. I don't like being brave. I don't like putting myself in situations where I don't know all the answers or have no indication of how the outcome is going to turn out. It causes me to stress out, freak out, make up a bajillion scenarios in my head about what could go wrong, and then my wigging out prevents me from taking the courageous steps that I know I need to take. That's what I love about this verse so much. It reminds me that I do not have to know all the answers about everything, only to know the *one* thing that can get me through any situation. My God is the God of the universe, the stars, all creation, and me. He knows me and is for me. I am not possibly powerful enough to screw up the plans He has for me, but that being said, I do need to rest my courage in Him, knowing that He's got me and is strong enough to work through me in times where I am fearful.

Learn to surrender. It is not your strength you must rely on when you feel less than or not enough for something, but God's strength in you that will get you through any obstacle that comes your way. Do you understand that your God has already put all the tools in your toolbox that you need, not just to get through any challenge, but to end up stronger because of it? That tool is Him. You have the God of the universe in your toolbox. I wonder how much more alive and bolder we would live if we truly believed that. What would we dare to dream if we knew that no dream was too big for the God that is for us? Because that is the truth. You will be scared, but do it scared. It doesn't matter whether you experience fear or not when it comes to facing the things you need to face in the pursuit of your dreams. What matters is that you continue to pursue your dreams relying on God's strength in you despite those fears.

God, give me the strength today to do it scared. Courage isn't the absence of fear; it is doing it despite all the fear I feel inside. Remind me all things are possible because I have your strength to rely on. Amen.

Tunnel Vision

> *'Let your eyes look straight ahead; fix your gaze directly before you"* Proverbs 4:25

Have you ever run on a treadmill and tried turning your head in all directions, looking everywhere to see everything? Of course not, that would be exhausting. Typically, you just get on a treadmill and look straight ahead, right? Turning your head side to side to look at everything you can possibly get a glimpse of would take away energy from the thing you are trying to accomplish, which is getting in a good run. So why do we do that in life? When it comes to our lives, instead of keeping our eyes on the truth that in Him we are enough, we spend our entire lives looking everywhere else for reasons as to why we are not. We spend our entire lives turning our heads, looking at other people and their opinions, clothes, places, judgments, attitudes, tones, salaries, children, accomplishments, and so on. When we spend our lives turning our head side to side, trying to see what everyone else's life looks like, we are taking away energy from the run of our own life.

You have got to have what my mom calls tunnel vision. Put your blinders on to the things around you that are distracting you from the thing you should be putting your focus on, which is Him. Live in that space of tunnel vision, block out the noise and chatter of other people's opinions and judgments, and keep looking forward at His promise. If you do that, you will follow the path and live as the person God created you to be on this earth. Keep your focus straight. Look to His promises. Stop wasting your energy, looking around at what everyone else is doing, and start living into the journey God called you to follow.

God, I pray you give me the humility I need today to recognize all the energy I was looking around at other people's lives. You have blessed me in a way that caters to the mission you need for me to fulfill on this earth. Help me use tunnel vision to see it and live into that promise.
Amen.

Remember Who Forgiveness is For

'll be honest, sometimes, it's really hard for me to forgive people. You know when someone just does you so incredibly wrong, and all you want to do is knock the stew out of them? I get that feeling a lot. Probably not very "Christian-sounding" of me to say, but it's the truth, and I want this to be a space where we can be honest.

The truth is that forgiveness is not an easy thing. I do not care how many bible verses you can say by heart or how much you go to church, when you are deeply hurt by someone, our human instinct is not to turn around and forgive that person. I feel as if we have it in our minds that the bigger and longer the grudge we hold against that person, the more we hold them in captivity from ever being released from their wrongdoing. Thing is, that is totally backward from what is actually the case. When you hold a grudge against someone, the only person you are holding captive from letting go of that situation is yourself. The other person may or may not get over it, but will you? When you don't forgive someone, you are preventing yourself from being freed of that situation and pain; it does nothing to them despite what you may think. You do not have the power to control whether or not someone feels sorry for something they did. What you do have power over, and what I encourage you to do for yourself, is make the choice to be free from being captive in that wrongdoing yourself. Holding a grudge against someone is like you handing them the chains for them to hold you down in that situation forever. Forgiveness is not about the other person; it is about you. When you forgive, you free yourself from having any weight of that situation holding you down.

God orders us to forgive, not for the other person's benefit, but for our own. He knows that if we hold a grudge, it will only do harm to us and our spirit, and He doesn't want that for us. That is why we are ordered to forgive other people first and foremost so that it can create a space for us to become open to the possibility of God forgiving us for our wrongdoings.

God, today I choose forgiveness. Whatever harm may come my way today, or that has in the past, I choose forgiveness. I do not want to be held captive by the self-inflicting chains of my past pains anymore. I forgive, help me forgive.
Amen.

Acknowledge Your Pain

> *"Do not be afraid or discouraged, for the Lord will personally go ahead of you. He will be with you; he will neither fail you nor abandon you."*
> Deuteronomy 31:8

I was listening to a podcast this morning about pain and how people are afraid to go to the places in their heart where that pain lies. Emotional numbing isn't something people just decide they are going to do one day, but it's something that you slowly become chained by over time. It's not like one day you just decide to numb out every single thing that has ever caused you pain in your life, but more along the lines of as you go throughout your life, certain things happen that you just don't want to bear the weight of those emotions from. As a result of all of this, you numb the emotions out.

The podcast was talking about when you numb out pain, sorrow, sadness, and hurt, you also are numbing out joy. You cannot numb certain emotions and not the others, so when you numb some, you numb the all. I don't know if you have seen the movie *Inside Out* (highly recommended, and yes, it is animated), but there is a reason the characters "sadness" and "joy" get lost together- you cannot have one without the other. So, when you try to numb out the parts of you that feel pain and hurt, you are also numbing the parts of you that experience joy and gladness.

Don't numb the pain you feel. I think the reason people numb it in the first place is that they are afraid of how much it'll hurt if they allow themselves to go there and to feel it all. The problem is that over time, numbing small things turns into numbing everything, and before you know it, the very thing you were trying to avoid- sadness/pain/depression/anger- is consuming you every single day because you also blocked out joy. God loves all parts of you. He loves the good, the bad, the sad, the ugly, the beautiful, the angry, the jealous, the pained, and the hurting. The parts of you that have it all figured out, and the parts of you that don't. Showing yourself the true pain that you feel is also showing God that pain. Take Him to that place. He is always with you and isn't going anywhere. He wants you to trust him with your pain.

Lord, here is my pain. Here are my burdens. I give them to you heavy-hearted, in hope to be released from the weight they carry that holds me down. Give me the strength to feel all that is in me, so that I can be most connected to you.
Amen.

Take the Road Less Traveled

> *"Enter through the narrow gate. For wide is the gate and broad is the road that leads to destruction, and many enter through it. But small is the gate and narrow is the road that leads to life, and only a few find it." Matthew 7:13-14*

'll admit it, there were a lot of times in my life where I didn't want to do the right thing. Now, what is the "right thing" you might ask? Well, for me, it's that thing that keeps nudging me in certain situations, telling me to do something other than what I want to do at that moment. For example, the other day, my sister and I called each other the royal B word because I was taking too long to go to Target. She got mad, and I lashed out, it ended in a verbal free for all. About an hour later, we were sitting in the same room, not speaking, of course, and I could just feel that "apologize, Annie" voice getting louder and louder in my head, nudging me to go tell my sister I was sorry, but I seriously didn't want to. I didn't want to give her that satisfaction, and knowing my sister, she wasn't about to apologize back to me even if I swallowed my pride and did it first. I wish I could type, here and now, that I listened to that voice and apologized, despite the aftereffects of my ego being crushed, but unfortunately, I cowered back and opted for a text-apology later that day.

You guys, sometimes doing the right thing is freaking hard, and you don't feel like it. That's why Jesus pointed out to His disciples that a majority of the people will not follow the path that leads to Christianity, because it's really hard. Funny enough, I was having this exact conversation with someone last night. Just how so many people have the misconception that when you give your life to Christ, all of a sudden, your life becomes easier in some sort of way. Sorry to burst your bubble, but that couldn't be further from the truth. If anything, things get more challenging. It is so much easier to go through life without a moral compass. Having to be conscious of doing the right thing all the time? That's really hard. Having to own up to your mistakes? It'd be so much easier to just numb them out. Having to love *all* people, even the ones you would categorize as your arch-nemesis? The most challenging thing someone in the human flesh can be asked to do. Yet, that is what we are called to do from our Father, and when you accept Him as your Savior, you are accepting that moral awareness. The thing I want you to know, though, is it is so worth it. Not everyone is going to continue down this narrow, long, empty path, simply because it isn't filled with the majority. Please, though, hear me say that you don't need the majority when you have His majesty. You have the King of all Kings walking right there beside you, keep going down the path. Narrow as it may be, that path will lead you to the place you want to end up.

God, give me the strength to stay on the path. The narrow path that leads to you is the only path that I need to be following, and I need you to give me the strength to stay off from the crowd and continue this journey with you. You and Your direction are all I need. Amen.

Stay In This Moment

> *"Therefore, do not be anxious about tomorrow, for tomorrow will be anxious for itself. Sufficient for the day is its own trouble." Matthew 6:34*

I am a to-do list kind of girl. There is nothing more satisfying than 1) making a to-do list and 2) crossing things off that to-do list. I do it every single morning when I am done with my workout, sitting down, and about to start my work for the day. It's just the incredible feeling of having all those responsibilities out of your head and onto a piece of paper that I love so much. Maybe you're the kind of person that can hold a bunch of information at once and not forget, but us mere mortals over here tend to forget information if it isn't written down or in some form that reminds us of the things we need to get done. I am one of those mere mortals. That being said, sometimes, I get so caught up in all the things I have to do that day, that while I am on one thing on my to-do list, my mind is already on the next thing. Actually, scratch that, my mind is already on the thing 5 things down the list from the thing I am currently on. Yes, it is good that I think ahead, but the downfall of this is that whatever task I am doing at this moment is compromised because my full attention and energy are not focused on it.

Something I have realized in life is that I tend to treat my life similarly to my to-do list. I am so busy yearning for a phase of my life that is a few years away from the one I am currently in that I tend to miss out on this very moment I am living in. You are currently in the very place of your life for a reason. There is something in this season that God is trying to teach you, and if you spend your entire life looking forward to the next thing, you're going to miss out on the lessons, gifts, blessings, and miracles that God is trying to give you in this season of life.

Start looking around at your life right now. Be in this moment. Stay in the present, because God is trying to teach you something right here and right now. Don't miss it.

God, I know that my life is going to be this incredible story that you are currently writing, but help my stay focused on this chapter. Sometimes my mind wants to skip ahead, and sometimes it wants to stay stuck in the past, help me center it to this moment so I can be fully present in the blessing that is now.
Amen.

Trust, Even When You Can't See

> *"Now faith is the assurance of things hoped for, the conviction of things not seen." Hebrews 11:1*

Let me tell you, it's really easy to praise God when everything is going right in your life. I have had days where it's almost as if every single little thing is going my way. My mom gave me a spare $20, I got an A on that exam, I had an amazing workout, the toast I thought I'd burned since I forgot about it in the toaster was toasted perfectly golden brown, I got the job offer, I closed the sale, I found an extra pack of bubblegum in my gym bag, and it basically felt as if anything that I could possibly label as something good, happened me to me that day. On those days, it is so easy to say, "the Lord is good," "God's got me," "He has a plan," and basically, anything that announces your trust in what He's got going on for your life. What's really hard to do is say the same things when you're down in the dumps. When you're in the valley, and all of a sudden, you can't see anything in front of you, it's really hard to say, "I know God's got a plan for me," with a lot of enthusiasm. However, my friends, it is in those moments that our conviction is the most tested, and our words of belief mean the most.

Anyone can say thank you on a day that they are receiving all the gifts they could possibly ask for, but that is not what we are called to do. We are called to say thank you for the things seen and unseen. Can you say thank you to God even when you cannot see the fruits that He has in store for you at this very moment? Even when His plan does not make sense? The beautiful thing about God is that He is the God of the hills and the valleys. In fact, one of my favorite songs ever is a song called "Hills and Valleys" by Taren Wells, and it touches on this exact concept. God sees us in both. He's with us in both. No matter where we are, He's with us, and He promises us that beautiful things are going to come from any and all situations we are in. Even in your valley, when you cannot see the view of the beautiful mountain God is going to get you to the top of, say thank you for the view that you know is coming. I saw God all the time, "Lord, thank you for all the good things I know are coming my way that I don't even see yet."

God, thank you. Thank you for the bad things and the good. Thank you for the easy things and the challenging. All of them are leading me to the fruit you have in store for me. Today I say thank you for it all and for seeing me in the hills and the valleys. I am never alone because I always have you. I pray you help me live in that reassurance.
Amen.

Get a New Perspective

> "So, we don't look at troubles we can see now; rather,
> we fix our gaze on things that cannot be seen. For the
> things we see now will soon be gone, but the things we
> cannot see will last forever."
> *2 Corinthians 4:18*

I have this workout app called "Workout Women," it's free, I highly suggest you get it because it is absolutely amazing. The other day in my quick 10-minute ab workout, I was complaining about how this app always played the same songs over and over again. Every single time I went in and did this workout, or the 10-minute glute workout, or the 10-minute HIIT workout, the same two songs played on a loop, and I was so tired of it. Yesterday, though, I did something I usually don't do; I tried a new workout. I tried one of the workouts that was 15 minutes, not 10, and guess what? The app played different songs for the 15-minute workout than the 10-minute ones I was doing. All the while, I was complaining that this app didn't do enough to diversify its musical output, I had no idea that it did, in fact, have a bunch of other songs, but they were in the workouts that I was avoiding.

Sometimes, in life, we blame and complain about why things are not going our way when what we are looking for is right there in front of us, we just need to be willing to get out of our "normal" and get a new perspective. What, in your life right now, are you wishing was different? Maybe you lack energy, perhaps, you hate your job, there is also the possibility you're at a place, right now, where your marriage or relationship isn't the strongest. I encourage not to "delete the app and get a new one," or in better terms, quit your job, your relationship, or your hopes for having energy throughout your day, instead, why don't you try to mix it up? Go into your work today with a new perspective, challenging yourself to find five things an hour that make you happy while at work (this could be as little as holding your warm coffee in your hands at your desk). Ask your partner to do a date night that you have never done before, maybe outside, on a picnic blanket, under the stars. Mix it up a little bit, and you will get a new perspective that doesn't require you to completely change the circumstances but strengthen the context of them that you are in.

God, I pray you give me a new perspective today. Help me fix my eyes on you and you alone to give me the strength I need to create the change in my life that will lead me closer to you.
Amen.

Where Do You Run To?

> "But those who hope in the Lord will renew their strength. They will soar on wings like eagles; they will run and not grow weary; they will walk and not be faint." Isaiah 40:31

There's been a lot of pain in my life that I have run away from. Figuratively and literally. Running, itself, has always been therapy for me, a time where I could think and reflect, but there was a point in my life where it was an escape from feeling the pain that I shoved deep down in my heart. I had this fear of not being good enough. It was a feeling that started after the boy I first gave my heart to decided to break up with me. I felt that it was my fault the relationship didn't work out, that somehow, I wasn't worthy or valuable enough of a person to make him stay. Instead of confronting these limiting beliefs, I just shoved them down. I didn't want to feel them because that would be too painful. So, I started running from them. Literally. I ran and ran and ran until I was averaging at least 12 miles a day plus, at the time, the practices I had for the sport I played in college, which was tennis. Running gave me confidence, purpose, and made me feel good. In my mind, I associated my achievements as a runner with being worthy as a person. Running was my way of escape.

For you, it might be different. Drugs, sex, alcohol, a relationship, work, homework, school, or gossip are all ways of escape that people have chosen to use before. The thing about these escapes is that they work for a little while. For a little while, sex does make you feel better. Drugs and alcohol do give you that high that masks the pain you shoved inside of you. However, they also lead to a larger crash than the one that caused your need for escape in the first place. The only way to heal that pain (and you're not going to like my answer)? Expose it. You have got to show it to God. Give your pain to Him. He wants us to give Him all that we are and to shine a light on the darkness that weighs heavily in our hearts. Put your hope of healing in Him, and you will be lifted higher than any short-term high could ever give you.

God, here is me. Pain, cracks, bruises, tears, breaks, and all. Use my pain for a purpose. I expose to you the darkness that has been weighing heavy on my heart for so long. Shine your light on it to expose and heal it.
Amen.

Power in the Waiting

> *"Let us not become weary in doing good, for at the proper time we will reap a harvest if we do not give up." Galatians 6:9*

Ever since I was in high school, I've had big dreams. I didn't know how, but I knew the world was going to hear from me in some way. My spirit at 16 years old wanted to do jump, leap, and boldly step into big things. The problem was that I just didn't know what that was yet. It was when I was 18 years old and at my first self-development conference for my nutrition company that I was finally poured into with the vision of what my life could look like and who I wanted to be. I saw a young girl speaking on stage, pouring into thousands of people, and I knew that was what I wanted to do with my life. I wanted to speak, teach, and pour into people all about God's goodness, love, and grace. How do I know that was my calling and not just a fleeting infatuation? Four years later, I still get up every single morning with that same intention. I want to serve. I want to lead. I want to speak the words that I know God put in my heart and pours into me with every single day.

Here's the thing, though, my friends. That hasn't happened yet. I haven't had the privilege of speaking to a crowd larger than 200 people, nor have I accumulated the massive following and reputation that comes with those invitations. Even though there is no rain right now, I am preparing for the Lord to bring the rain at some point. That is the purpose of waiting, in my opinion. The waiting sucks, but if you were given everything you ever dreamed of in a split second, there would be no story for you to tell. Kevin Hart once talked about how it is in the waiting of your dreams, that the story you will tell once you achieve your dreams lies. The success of your dreams is determined by how well you prepare for them before you have any physical evidence they are going to come true. How you prepare in the wait is a testimony to your faith. Keep going every day, preparing for the Lord to fulfill the dreams He has placed in your heart, whether it be 1 year, 2, years, or 20 years. Keep going.

Lord, I am right here and right now, and the fruition of my dreams is nowhere in sight. I will keep going and going because I know you put this dream on my heart for a reason. Help me use this waiting time to prepare for all You have in store.
Amen.

Open the Grave, I'm Coming Out

>>> →

"And they found the stone rolled away from the tomb,
but when they went in, they did not find the body of
Lord Jesus" Luke 24:2-3

There's a song by Elevation Worship called "Rattle." In this song, it has a line that reads, "open the grave, I'm coming out, I'm going to live, going to live again." Sometimes in life, I feel like I am at the end of the road. It feels like the weight of all of my insecurities, doubts, depressive thoughts, anxiety, and uncertainty is taking over everything that God says is true in my life. This past semester, my senior year of college, there were mornings that I had the chance to sleep in, but my anxiety woke me up so early that I couldn't fall back asleep. I was scared of the future, and the lack of a certain plan for it, and I was also dealing with this fear of never being good enough for the people in my life that I want to make proud.

There are moments where my life has taken unexpected

turns, or things have happened that I wasn't planning on, and I just feel buried, maybe you've felt the same. Remember, at those moments where you feel like the inside of you is completely dead or dying, God beat death. Jesus beat death. Open that grave of yours that tells you that you aren't good enough, worthy, loved, or capable, and come out! God came to resurrect Jesus not to declare for one single day that death is defeated, but all death is defeated for eternity. This isn't just the physical means of death, but the feelings in your heart that are killing you every single day. Depression. Anxiety. Unworthiness. Fear. Doubt. Uncertainty. All the feelings that come after and try to kill you have been defeated with Jesus! Open your grave, YOU are coming out today.

God, you beat death for me. Every single day is an opportunity to get up, open the grave my anxiety is trying to put me in, and come out to the world, showing every bit of my spirit that I can.
Amen.

Redefine Success

When I wrote my first book, *Be Your Own Hero*, I defined the success of it by the number of copies it sold. I would constantly check how many copies it was selling, and if it sold less that week than the previous week, I would feel as if my book was a failure. I imagined every week it would increase in sales until, eventually, it would be on the New York Times bestsellers list- I am a dreamer, what can I say. Looking back, to think that I'd hit the NYT Bestsellers list after having written just one book was a slight bit egotistical, but that was the dream placed in my heart. I defined the success of that book by how many copies were sold. I defined the success by a numerical value in the slot on the website labeled "sales this week." Later that semester, I read a chapter of my book that I'd dedicated to the woman, who, alongside my parents, raised my siblings and me. I dedicated this chapter to this woman because it was all about joy, and Gwen was the epitome of joy. When I read her the chapter, she started crying because it meant so much to her. I wanted that chapter to communicate to people, and to Gwen, herself, just how powerful of a person she was in my siblings and my lives. At that moment, where I shared with her the reading of this chapter, seeing those tears in her eyes, hearing her say how much she loved me, and knowing I had the chance to communicate with her how much she meant to us, I realized that this book was a success. Even if it wasn't a New York Times bestseller, it impacted one person. It showed my Genny how much she meant to us, and that was all the means of success I could ever ask for.

Your initial definition of success may not be the standard God is holding your achievements to. You may not be number one in your med school, but did going through med school change your heart and incline you closer to Him? Then you were successful. You may not have gotten the Golden Globe Award, but in the process of going for it, did you learn more about yourself and faith? Then you were successful. I realized that success lies in the pursuit, not the accomplishment. Did you become a better person because of your pursuit? Did your heart change and incline itself toward the Lord? If so, you were successful.

God, I know my initial definition of success may not be the means to which you define all that I am doing. Help me see the success I have already established and will continue to, in the process.
Amen.

Separate and Appreciate

> *"Or am I seeking the approval of man, or of God?*
> *Or am I trying to please man? If I were still trying*
> *to please man, I would not be a servant of Christ."*
> *Galatians 1:10*

In the mornings, I have gotten in the good habit of avoiding the "scroll-hole." You know the hole I am talking about? That deep, dark, barren pit of comparison you find yourself in when you first wake up and comb through the latest Instagram posts, Snapchat stories, FB shares, or Tiktok creations. It's so easy just to pull out your phone and start scrolling, waking up from your scroll-hole blackout 30 minutes later, forgetting what it is you were even looking at. Social media makes it so easy to start feeling absolute crap about ourselves. We compare ourselves behind the scenes to someone else's highlight reel, and before we know it, our life seems like a failure compared to that other person's.

So yes, in the mornings, I am protective over what I

consume and my energy, so I refuse to go on social media until I have done the things that fill my cup with goodness, like the Bible, a good personal growth book, and journaling.

Have you ever been in a situation where you were feeling really good about yourself, then all of a sudden, you saw a post of someone else who did something amazing or was looking amazing, and in a matter of two seconds, you went from feeling good to feeling crappy about yourself? I used to do this with my body image. I would feel in shape, fit, and confident, then I saw a girl on Instagram looking amazing in a photo on the beach, and all of a sudden, I felt crappy about my own body because it didn't look like "hers." Anyone else experience something like this? I want to remind you that someone else's accomplishments, looks, or features do not take away from your own. In fact, they have nothing to do with one another. The only way the two become connected is when you start comparing yourself to that person. There is a practice I wrote about in my first book called "separate and appreciate." When you find yourself comparing, remember you are separate from that person you are comparing yourself to. Who they are or what they've done doesn't take away from who you are or what you've done? Once you have separated the two, you can appreciate the other person for whatever it is they have done or who they are. If you spend your entire life comparing yourself to other people, you will miss out on the miracle God created you to be.

God, you made me, me, for a reason. Help me stop comparing myself to all of these other people and start appreciating the one of a kind masterpiece that is me. Amen.

Say Thank You, Twice

> "Give thanks in all circumstances; for this is God's
> will for you in Christ Jesus."
> 1 Thessalonians 5:18

Sometimes it's hard to say thank you to God when you feel like nothing in your life is going the way you want it; I'll be the first to say it. If you were hoping for a devotional that was written by someone who was genetically wired to always see the good and never be upset, even in the midst of a battle, sorry friend, you've come to the wrong devotional. I want to be real with you guys, though. It is hard. Sometimes I do get upset, and I do get impatient because I have all of these dreams in my heart that I know God gave me, and it just feels like He's hanging me out to dry. There's a point in every journey where nothing is happening on the surface, so it's easy to think that nothing is happening at all. I want to talk to you today as someone who has to remind herself of this every single day- that isn't true.

When you give your heart to God and sing His praises, it means so much more than you just saying "thank you" when everything in your life is perfect; it means also saying "thank you" when everything is going not as you initially pictured it would. I think when we say thank you, we really need to be saying thank you twice, once for all the things we can see that God has done in our life and the second time for all the things we cannot. All the challenges, heartbreaks, obstacles, and pains that God has protected us from that we don't even know about. All the events that could have led to long nights, anxiety, tears, and wounds that God protected us from going through. When you thank God tonight in your prayers for all the things in your life that you can see, remember to thank Him too for the things you cannot. When things in your life don't look the way you thought they would turn out, or you are feeling like God has left you out to dry because nothing seems to be going right in your life, perhaps God is using this season to protect you from things you don't even know were a threat to you in the first place. Say thank you twice.

God, thank you for all the things you have put and protected me from in my life. Thank you, thank you. I thank you twice, even though it should be so many times more.
Amen.

Tell 'Em Who You Are

> "Do not be conformed to this world, but be transformed by the renewal of your mind, that by testing you may discern what is the will of God, what is good and acceptable and perfect." Romans 12:2

My entire life, I have wanted to please people. I can remember being a little girl and wanting to please my parents more than anything. Even little things, like when my mom would say, "oh this is such a special one," after giving her an ornament for her to hang on the tree, lit me up inside because I was the one to hand her that particular ornament she loved so much. This caused some intense Christmas tree decorating sessions because my siblings and I would always try to be the first to get my mom her favorite ornaments. If you asked them about this, they probably didn't remember it as a competition, but the people pleaser in me absolutely did. I wanted to be the one who got praise for giving her the special ornaments.

Now that I can see clearly just how much people pleasing

has bled into my life and taken over a lot of my behaviors, it's easy for me to identify when my actions are falling prey to this previously conditioned behavioral pattern I had. I used to do everything to please other people, even at the expense of my own happiness. I wanted everyone to like me. I want to remind you of something that took me years to figure out, and something I still have to remind myself of every day- it is impossible to please everyone. Literally impossible. You might as well do what makes you happy because there will always be someone that doesn't agree with what you do, even if you think what you're doing *is* going to please everyone, I assure you it is not. You've got to define who you are and who you want to be in this world, or the world will define it for you by default. If you aren't intentional about what makes you happy, and act on that thing, the world will tell you it is stupid, and you should do something else. Do what makes you happy. Live your life filled with all your passions. Create abundance in your everyday routine. People disagree with you for it. Guess what, there will also be people who do support you. It's just how the world works. Everyone has their own viewpoint and is going to see you differently. You must ask yourself, how do *you* want to see *yourself*?

God, give me the strength today to be completely me.
No apologies. No regrets. No hesitation. I want to show
up as the person you created me to be, flaws and all.
Amen.

Set Your Boundaries

> *"For each will have to bear his own load."*
> *Galatians 6:5*

I have learned something recently- it's better to know your boundaries and set them than to let the world set them for you. It's okay to set boundaries and not apologize for them. For the longest time, I use to think that I always had to be ready on call for all people and all opportunities, but at the end of the day, I always felt exhausted because I was spending all my attention on what everyone else wanted me to do, instead of what I wanted to do. Is there a balance? Absolutely. Sometimes we have to do things we don't necessarily want to do, but there are also boundaries we must set for ourselves and honor so that when we do show up to the things we do every day, we are authentically pouring into that situation the most that we can.

Recently, I accepted an invitation to the beach with a couple of girlfriends. As soon as I said yes, I knew I'd made a mistake. Not because of my girlfriends- they are some of the most incredible friends I could ask for in my life, but simply because I know myself, and I am not a "trip" kind of friend. I am the friend that likes to have dinner with you, go on walks with you, you have an emergency? I'm there. You want to facetime for an hour? Let's do it. A trip, though? I am someone that likes my alone time and routine schedule way too much for trips. This is something I know about myself, so much so, that it is a boundary I have set for myself. I know that I go on trips with friends, and I get so stressed out by the lack of a schedule, routine, alone-time, I become the opposite of good company. That being said, the reason I said yes is that I totally did not honor my boundaries and had a serious case of FOMO (fear of missing out) when all my friends started talking about it. The further I thought after I accepted the invitation, though, the more I realized that not only would I not be having fun, but that would 100% affect my friends' good time too. So, I told them the truth, and they completely understood. That's the thing, you guys, we all have boundaries. Some of us need mornings to ourselves, and sometimes we need evenings; some of us protect our sleep like a mama bear and its cub. It is good to have boundaries and to honor them. In fact, in doing that, I truly believe you are honoring not only yourself but he people in your life. When you honor your boundaries, you start to show up as a more full, authentic, and energized person that has it in them to love more openly and in the way your loved ones deserve.

God, you gave me my boundaries for a reason, help me honor them. Though sometimes it is hard and difficult, help me see the importance of them to show up as my fullest self.
Amen.

Trust the Process

> *"And endurance produces character, and character produces hope. Romans 5:4*

All throughout my collegiate tennis career, my coach was in love with the phrase, "trust the process." She loved this phrase so much that we had customized shirts made with this logo on the back for all to see. Whenever I was upset or frustrated, she would just say, "trust the process, trust the process." At the time, I absolutely had no idea what she meant, and looking back, I can see how I didn't because tennis was no longer a dream or a passion of mine. However, when I apply that phrase to the current dreams and desires, I have in my heart, I can see why she felt that phrase was so powerful.

Imagine if we just suddenly got everything that we wished for; if all of our dreams came true at the click of a button, and we never had to work for anything to get to where we dreamed of being. Sure, the forefront of that imaginary scenario sounds fantastic. However, if you really think about it, that takes away all of the specialness of that dream. What makes an achievement so great is the work that goes into accomplishing it. The long nights, early mornings, times you didn't feel like doing it but did it anyway, the rainy days, the sunny days, and all of the adversity presented to you in going for your dream is what makes the achievement so special. That is why, when you do come across adversity, hardships, obstacles, or challenge, you must remember that success isn't a destination, it is a journey. The process of getting to that achievement is the true achievement in itself. All the lessons learned, and strength acquired, is the thing you should be most proud of and what should be held dearest in your heart. Wherever you are in the journey toward your dream at the moment, trust the process you are currently in.

God, I pray that you remind me to trust my current process. The miracle is not in a destination, but in the everyday lessons and strength I am gaining from the process You are taking me through. Help me to see that, embrace it, and lean into it.
Amen.

See It Through

I am only 22 years old. That being said, there is a lot of my life (I hope) that I have yet to live and thus, a lot of things I have yet to learn. However, I will say that in my 22 years, there is one lesson about success that I know for a fact is true for all the people that have ever achieved their dreams or have accomplished something most people only dream about- they give it enough time. So many people fall prey to the "microwave society" thinking. This idea that we can pop our dreams in the microwave and have them come out in 15 minutes filled with success, praise, and pride. I am sorry to break it to you that it doesn't work like that. Great things take time. They take hard work. Yes, I know I am preaching to the choir here because you have probably heard this your entire life. The problem is that common sense isn't always common practice. You can know something but not *know* it at the same time. Yes, I am sure you have heard that anything worth having takes time and work, but it still amazes me how soon people quit on their dreams after they start pursuing them.

Tony Robbins says that people overestimate what they can do in a year and underestimate what they can do in a decade. You have got to stay the course, my friend. That dream you want so badly. Keep going. Get up even when you don't feel like it. Do that little, simple, small thing that will take you one step closer toward your goal every single day. You have got to just see your dream through. Steven Furtick says it best when he talks about how going after your dreams requires two "yes's." The first is the yes to the idea of your dream. The second is the yes you continue to say when you are pursuing your dreams and adversity arises, yet you keep going. The second yes is what matters most. Anyone can start, what matters is who finishes. You want to be the one that finishes the dream and sees it through, not just the one that says they are going to start something and then quits when it gets hard. Keep going. See it through.

God, help me see this dream you planted on my heart through. You gave me all my dreams for a reason, give me the strength to say yes twice. Yes, to the idea of it, and yes, right in the middle of the obstacles that will arise in the pursuit of it.
Amen.

Step On Out

"Trust in the Lord with all your heart, and do not lean on your own understanding. In all your ways acknowledge him, and he will make straight your paths." Proverbs 3:5-4

Right now, I am mixing up my workouts. I am a cardio girl at heart, and this new "weightlifting" thing is absolutely throwing me off my rocker. I know it is important for me, but I feel so uncomfortable doing it. All I want to do is go back to the treadmill and run. I can honestly say it's not so much that I love running that much, I do love it a lot, but more because I just feel more comfortable doing it than weightlifting. Even though combining the two in my regimen would be more beneficial for my health and energy, the discomfort of trying weightlifting makes me not want to do it.

It's funny how we do this so often in life. Even though we know something is good for us, we refrain from doing it because it is uncomfortable. People will spend their entire lives in a miserable yet familiar place rather than strive for a better circumstance that is unfamiliar. They don't like being uncomfortable. The problem with this is that to stay in our comfort zone suggests we think we know everything that is good for us, which we do not. God knows what is good for us, and He gives us opportunity after opportunity in our lives that we continuously turn down because it is unknown territory. I cannot tell you how many times I knew I needed to change up my workout routine and add weights, but I resisted because I didn't even know where to begin. Now that I have been doing it a few weeks, I can't believe I went all that time without it! I feel so much better and stronger. It took me surrendering to an unknown and unfamiliar opportunity to get a better result than I was experiencing in my comfort zone. What in your life are you holding yourself back from because you're afraid of the unknown? Remember that we aren't supposed to know everything; that's God's job. Our job is to simply show up to the opportunities He placed in our lap, even if they are unfamiliar.

Lord, give me the strength to surrender my need for control to you today I give you all that I have, and I hope that I answer every opportunity you have come knocking on my door with a willing attitude to try something new
Amen.

Keep Your Focus

➤———————→

> *"Let your eyes look directly forward, and your gaze may be straight before you." Proverbs 4:25*

I was listening to a sermon from Steven Furtick this morning, and something that he said really struck me. He talked about how if the enemy could have killed you by now, he would have. The enemy isn't strong enough to take you down. He can't when you have God on your side, fighting your battles for you. Since the enemy can't kill you, he'll go after the next best thing- your focus. The reality of it is that whatever we focus on, becomes what makes us up every single day. Our focus dictates our thoughts, which, in return, drives our actions and behaviors. The enemy will try and distract you from the purpose God put on your life so that you won't end up following it. The enemy will use your thoughts to try and discourage you away from the thing God is calling you to do so that you won't do it.

Have you ever had that thing in your heart you know

God put there and is calling you toward, but "life" just keeps getting in the way, and you never get around to it? It's that thing that if you did, you know it would change everything, but because you are comfortable in your miserable but familiar day to day circumstances, you simply put up with your current situation instead of doing that one thing that could change it because you keep getting distracted? That's how the enemy stops God's work from coming into this world. The enemy can't stop God putting greatness into us, but he can stop us from focusing on that greatness.

The next time you know in your gut there is that thing you are meant to do, listen to it. Even if it is just one action item you identify and take, do it. Make it a priority. If you don't, the enemy will have, yet again, accomplished distracting someone out of the greatness that God placed in their heart and in their life. Stay focused on Him and Him alone. A lot of times, the day to day distractions are put there intentionally to lead you away from your greatness.

Lord, I am coming to you today as someone who struggles with getting distracted by all the things around me. Help me to keep my eyes on you and you alone, so that I can live into the purpose you have placed on my life.
Amen.

Conquer the Storm

Do you ever wonder how people who seem to be going through the worst of storms, still show up every day with a smile? As if they are still the most joyful and happy people in the world? Someone very dear to me in my life, who passed away earlier this year, was one of those people. My Gwenny. Gwen was the most joyful person alive. She suffered from a disease called pulmonary fibrosis, but even on her worst days, you wouldn't know how much pain she was in. Gwenny always showed up with a smile, a laugh, and a welcoming posture that could make anyone feel like the most special person in the world. Gwenny knew something about joy that took me forever to figure out- it is always in your control if you choose to focus on the right thing.

Much like how, when Peter's focus was on Jesus, he found himself walking on top of the storm, but the minute he took his eyes off Jesus and onto the stormy waters and wind, he started sinking. The key to how people can go through storms and not sink is because they are choosing not to let that storm permeate the vessel that is their heart. When a storm starts entering the boat, and the water gets in the bow, that is when the boat starts to sink. However, if the water never gets in the boat, even in the darkest of storms, the boat will float through it. That is just like our hearts. When we experience a storm in our life, if we focus on all the bad, it is like a boat allowing all the water from the storm to creep in and cause it to sink. Focusing on the good won't take you out of the storm, but it will keep you afloat so you can still show up and do what God has called you to do, which is to love people. Focusing on the good means focusing on the source of all joy- your Heavenly Father. In your storm that you're going through in your life right now, put your focus on Him. You won't sink in it.

God, help me put my focus on you in this storm. I can't change this storm, I can't get out of it, but I can choose my focus in it. I choose you. I choose joy. I choose your light. Give me the strength to shift my focus to you so I can stay afloat in this storm.
Amen.

Celebration in the Unseen

> *"Can a man hide himself in secret places so that I cannot see him? Declares the Lord. Do I not fill heaven and earth? Declares the Lord."* Jeremiah 23:24

Sometimes, I struggle with wanting to do good things. Yes, go ahead and judge me as a horrible person, but it's true. I feel like our entire world only celebrates the things that people see and can celebrate you for. That being said, it makes it hard to want to do things in the moments there are no people to praise you for it. I don't know if this is just me, but I feel like the moments where an opportunity arises for me to do something good for others, and there are no people around to praise me for it, I need a little extra push to want to do it. It's because, as a society, we have been drilled to think that if there is no photo of the act, no one around to see it happen, to celebrate you on social media or give you an Insta story shoutout, then it might as well not have happened.

I want to remind you that God sees it all. He sees the good that you do even when no one is around. He sees your kindness to others even when no one is there to tell you that you are acting kind. He sees the donations that you make anonymously, the people you give a ride to, the children you are simply loving toward, even when there is no one taking a picture of it to put on social media. God sees it all. People do not celebrate what is not seen, but God does. I want to tell you today that your Father saw. He saw those sleepless nights that you lay awake and didn't know that next step to take, He saw the moments you were doubtful and upset but showed up with a smile anyway, He saw the times you donated even when you barely had means to provide for yourself, He saw it all. He celebrates it all. You don't need to have it posted on social media to experience the satisfaction that your good deed was seen and noticed by the one that holds the ultimate reward. He sees the things you do that you feel no one else notices or appreciates. He sees it all.

Lord, remind me that you see it all. Even when I feel like nothing that I do is appreciated or seen, You are up there cheering me on and celebrating me. My ultimate reward is with You, and only You.
Amen.

Fail Forward

think we live in a world that not only fears failure but avoids it. People would rather not even try for a dream that rests in their heart than try and fail. I have a lot of dreams in my heart, and I will be completely honest. Sometimes, there is a part of me that swells up inside and tells me to stop. It tells me to stop while I'm ahead because if I keep going, I could fail, and failure would be worse than never going for it in the first place. Every day, I have to challenge that thinking. I know God put big dreams in my heart, and I have to remind myself that I would rather live my life in pursuit of dreams that will never come than live my life in pursuit of nothing at all. That's the thing about failure- it teaches you. Failure is the greatest lesson because it shows you the areas that you need to strengthen. Failure also reminds you of your humanity. Imagine if everything went perfectly for us all the time. Every single time we fail, it brings us back to the realization that we are only human, and I believe with all we get in that experience, we strengthen our relationship with our Creator.

I don't care what your dream is, but you need to act on it. In school, we were taught to study for weeks before a test. We were taught to practice and prepare to perfection before action. Life doesn't work like that. To be successful in life and the pursuit of your calling, you must constantly be acting. You learn as you go, and you fail forward. When you fall down, you learn what went wrong, adjust, correct it, and get back up. The path to success isn't a straight line. It looks more like a line that dips every so often but overall is progressing. In the pursuit of your dreams, if you're doing it right, you will fall. Falling and failing just indicates that you are challenging yourself to grow in areas you have not yet mastered, and that is a good thing. Failure is not a deviance from success but a prerequisite. I guarantee that the worst feeling in the world is not falling on your face in the pursuit of your dreams, it's regretting that you never pursued them at all. Get up, act, learn as you go, and fail forward. God is with you through every dark moment of failure, lighting your way closer to Him.

God, remind me that failure is the ultimate teacher.
It is the ultimate tool that can teach me how to
continuously reach for the best version of myself that
you need me to be to mark this world with the dreams
you put on my heart.
Amen.

The Truth About Unity

> *"For by Him all things were created, in heaven and on earth, visible and invisible, whether thrones or dominions or rulers or authorities- all things were created through Him and for Him. And He is before all things, and in Him all things hold together."*
> Colossians 1:16-17

Unity does not mean uniformity. Right now, there is a lot of hatred being multiplied in this world, and in particular, my country, the United States. I am a white, heterosexual female that is 22 years old. I say that because there are a lot of privileges in my life I have had simply because I have not been exposed to the kind of hatred other people of different minorities, sexualities, races, genders, religions, and ethnicities experience on a day to day basis. What scares me the most are the people that say, "they don't see color," or "they don't see gender." I fear these people because therein lies the problem. To begin a solution, we must expose light on the root of the situation, which is that people are in denial of the fact, at the core, not everyone's the same. We were not made to be the same. God did not make us all to be exactly alike. We are supposed to have different skin tones, opinions, beliefs, backgrounds, thoughts, ideas, sexualities, and parts that identify us as different genders. All things He makes are beautiful. We are all beautiful, but we are also all different. Uniting is not about saying everyone is the same, it is about accepting the totality of each person. It is saying, "I am different from you, you are different from me, and I accept you." It is believing that every part of you that is similar to someone else is just as beautiful as the parts of you that are different from someone else. It is accepting all the pieces of another human being who has experienced and gone through things you could never possibly understand and listening to those experiences instead of ignoring them.

We need to reach out our hearts to one another to understand the hearts of one another. People of different backgrounds and experiences need to listen to those experiences of other people. We need to unite, not in means to make everyone the same, but to unite in a way where everyone can see the differences in others and continue to accept all of them.

Lord, I pray for unity. I pray that we can all see and celebrate the differences of other people for exactly as they are- indications of the power that lies in your ability to create. Your creation ability is not limited to one type of person. You have the ability to create an abundance of different types of people. Help me speak and live this into our world.
Amen.

Prepare to Receive

> *"Prepare your work outside; get everything ready for yourself in the field, and after that build your house."*
> *Proverbs 24:27*

Full disclosure: when I am eating my avocado toast around 1 pm each day, I also look up a quick, 5-minute motivational video to watch. Today's motivational video was brought to me by none other than Steve Harvey, one of the funniest and inspirational people on this planet. He told the story of how he planned on getting a new car, but in his driveway, he had an old car he was keeping around that took up the entire space. His mom told him that until he moved that old car out of the driveway, he wasn't going to get a new car because he wasn't prepared to receive a new car with this old piece of junk taking up the entire space. He decided to get rid of his old car, opening up space in his driveway for this new car he hadn't found yet and wasn't sure he would ever find. Two weeks later, he found the car he loved and could afford.

There are so many times in our lives we pray to God to give us something that we are not prepared to receive. We have all this junk taking up space in our hearts, that even if God gave us the thing we were praying for, we would have no room to feel it in the way God intends for us. Maybe it's time to get rid of that old car you're carrying. Clear up some space. How do you expect God to put Mr. or Mrs. Right in your life if you're wasting your time with somebody that you know you don't have a future with? How do you expect God to land you your dream position at work if all you do is show up to work complaining about your current position? We must prepare to receive. Clear away old mentalities, behaviors, mindsets, and attitudes that are no longer serving you, so that you can make yourself available to receive the better things God has in store to give you.

God, help me get rid of all the old junk I am carrying in my heart. I know you have good things in store for me. I know that you are waiting until I am prepared to receive them to give them to me. Help me take the first steps in preparation.
Amen.

Tune Out the Noise

> *"So, faith comes through hearing, and hearing through the word of Christ."* Romans 10:17

There's a lot of noise in our world today. Noise from other's opinions, social media, news stations, professors, parents, friends, coaches, fellow peers, bosses, employees, employers, teachers- literally every direction you could ever possibly go in, there is going to be noise that finds you. In a world with so much noise, sometimes it is really hard to know what to listen to; to know who to listen to. Right now, in the United States, there are tons of riots going on for the Black Lives Matter movement. It is a seriously hard time, filled with struggle, pain, sorrow, and sadness. There are a lot of opinions circling around what is going on right now, and sometimes it can get really overwhelming. In times where I feel very overwhelmed, or do not know how to feel, I always remember that I am called to listen to my heavenly Father and only Him. It is so easy for us to drown in the noise from the world around us. It is such a slippery slope down toward becoming consumed by social media, Instagram likes, Facebook post reshares, what others think of you, how much money you have, and what people do or don't say about who you are. Remember that we are not called to be responsible for listening to any of the noise that is constantly around us, but instead, the sound of our Heavenly Father that lies within us, always. When we stop hearing and feeling the truth of the gospel is when we start tuning out the sound of faith and tuning into the sound of the world. It should always be the other way around. We must start tuning into our faith, and as a side effect, the volume of outside noise of the world will start to decrease. We've got to stay connected to His voice in us. Sit. Breathe. Close your eyes. His voice never left you; you just couldn't hear it because the volume of the world was louder. Get connected back to that inner voice, the voice of His truth. It sounds a lot like peace.

Lord, help me tune into You and only You. There is no other noise that will give me what my heart needs to hear.
Amen.

Teachers Learn Best

> *"Not many of you should become teachers, my fellow believers, because you know that we who teach will be judged more strictly" James 3:1*

I've heard it over and over again- teachers learn best. I don't think I ever truly understood this until it came to a point where I was taking on the role of "teacher" in a situation. Something I never realized until I heard it on Oprah's podcast was that whether we consciously assume the role of teacher or not, we are all teachers. No matter what we do, we teach other people how to treat and respect us by the way we treat and respect ourselves. Think about it. If you don't keep your commitments to yourself, do you really think other people are going to keep their commitments to you? If you don't appreciate your own time and take it seriously, are other people going to take you and your time seriously? We are always teaching other people how to treat us simply by the way we are treating ourselves every single day.

Needless to say, there are definitely circumstances where that is not the case, and some people treat us like crap even if we don't ourselves, but for a majority of the time, people take cues on how you treat yourself and reciprocate that cue back to how they treat you.

When you are going through hard times, remember to continue to treat yourself with patience, grace, and love. This will teach others to do the same for you and them. Also, know that how you overcome the hardships you are facing right now will someday be someone else's survival guide. The beauty of all hardships is that we can learn from them and grow them, and at some point, after them, use the lessons we gathered to help someone going through something similar. I remember after my first heartbreak during college, two girls reached out to me when they had their first relationship heartbreaks to learn about how I handled it. The hardships you are facing now will be the foundation for the lesson you will teach someday to someone going through something similar.

Lord, thank you for my battles. Through each, you teach me a new lesson, give me a deeper realization, and lead me closer to you. Help me not just overcome my battles, but not be afraid to learn from them, so eventually I can serve others going through similar tribulations.
Amen.

Trust Your Instinct

> "If any of you lacks wisdom, let him ask God, who gives generously to all without reproach, and it will be given him." James 1:5

Have you ever been in a situation where you literally have no idea what to do, and someone tells you to simply "trust your gut?" I don't know about you, but I have been there more times than I can count. All you want to do is just yell at them, "I don't even know what my gut is telling me!"

I remember one time, in particular, I was feeling this way. I had been dating this guy for almost a year and a half, and something just didn't feel right. It wasn't that I was unhappy, I just felt like there could be something more in a relationship. Naturally, I started asking literally every family member and friend I knew for advice because I didn't know what to do- to leave the relationship or not. I loved this guy, but something just didn't feel right. After having asked everyone that was closest to me, I felt more confused than ever. It was like the more information and input I got, the less clear things became.

We do that a lot in life. The minute we feel uncertain or unsure, we ask around to get the answers we think we are looking for. The reality is this usually leaves us making rash decisions, and more confused than ever. That gut feeling I talked about earlier. No wonder we don't know what our gut is telling us most of the time because we aren't listening! We are too busy listening to everyone else. When you don't know what to do, you've got to get still. You've got to get quiet. Oprah said it best when she said, "when you don't know what to do, do nothing." The reality is all the answers you need are already inside you, given to you by your Father. Stop asking Instagram, your mom and dad (no offense to them), best friend Susie, sister Lena, and start asking your God first. When you don't know what to do, give it a few days of just thinking about it with yourself and talking to Him before involving other people. You'd be surprised how smart those "gut feelings" really are once you actually listen to them.

God, you already have all the answers I could ever need on what to do. Help me cry out to you in times of uncertainty first, and not the people or media outlets around me. You've got all the wisdom I need.
Amen.

He Already Knows

You ever have that feeling of "oh crap," I have no idea what is coming next? Maybe you are at a point in your life where you feel like you just don't know what to do. Your parents want one thing from you, your significant other wants another, and your heart is telling you something totally different. I have moments like that at times. Funny enough, whenever I am feeling utterly confused and have no idea what to do, I find myself a closet, sit down, and just think. Not even kidding you. The closet for me is a space that triggers massive "thinking" mode, where I just talk to God and myself.

I think many of us, in times of uncertainty, start praying to God as if we have to remind Him of our situation. We pray with the intention of informing God about our troubles and what lies heavy on our heart instead of realizing God already knows every little thing that is going on. He knows what has happened in the past, what is happening now that is causing us so much grief, and what is coming at us in the future. We don't need to *inform* God when we speak to Him in times of trouble, we need to *involve* Him. Stop talking to Him like you're reminding Him of an appointment He's got with you that you think He's forgotten. Stop rehashing every single detail because you feel like He's forgotten the valley you are in- He already knows. Start expressing to Him what you are feeling. Start treating Him like the God of the universe that He is and expect the truth that He already has a solution for your problem and knows about it. Sometimes the valleys are there for us not to inform God we are in a valley, but for us to make the decision to walk in faith and realize God knows all things we are going through and already has the plan for the way out. I think that God wants us first to not just say He's the God that can move mountains but act in that belief by casting our worries about how we are going to get out of a valley onto Him. When we start moving in faith, He starts doing the things in our life that we are praying for.

God, you already know my pain, my weaknesses, my uncertainties. Help me move in faith. Help me involve you in my pain, not inform you. You already know; you don't need to be informed. Strengthen me to walk in this faith that I have for you.
Amen.

Dark Room God

> "But if we hope for what we do not see, we wait for it with patience." Romans 8:25

I am a huge fan of social media. I think it is a powerful tool that can create connections, friendships, networks, promote inspirations, generate ideas, and leverage a lot of good into our world. That being said, social media is exactly that- a tool, and just like any other tool, if it is used for the wrong thing, it can be very detrimental and harmful. Think about a hammer. A hammer can build houses, but it can also break bones if used incorrectly, and social media is no different.

I am afraid that because of social media, we have been conditioned into thinking that everything in our life has to be "Instagram perfect." We forget that life wasn't made to look like the perfectly edited, captioned, and filtered photos you see on someone else's highlight reel. Life is messy. Life isn't filtered. Life doesn't have a perfectly edited caption for it. Life can hurt sometimes. Life can take directions that you didn't anticipate or have a preset ready for when the snapshot of it happened. I am also afraid that we, as people, now think our dreams are supposed to happen as fast as a photo can be uploaded onto these social media platforms. We no longer want to dedicate years of our lives chasing a dream, we want our dream to happen *now*. Here's the thing- we don't have an Instagram God; we have a dark room God. Have you ever seen a photo get made in a dark room? It goes through several weeks of processing before it even turns up on the page. The dreams God placed in your heart are going to have to go through the same process. Stop expecting your dreams to pop up and appear, ready to be edited and filtered, then posted, all in less than 5 minutes. Your dreams are not Instagramable- they are a dark room feat. God will put that dream in your heart and then let it sit there while you go through life, grow, process, and learn, all so that the dream comes into fruition at exactly the right moment. Stop expecting your dream to come true tomorrow if you just thought of it today. Dreams take time to build, craft, process, and come alive. Be patient. You have a dark room God. Just because it doesn't look like on the surface anything is happening, it doesn't mean it isn't happening underneath. Your wait might just be the most crucial point of your journey- where God is strengthening you underneath.

God, I need you. I need you to remind me that this dream you put on my heart is there for a reason. I need you to give me the strength to remind myself that even though at the surface it may seem like nothing is happening, the most important processing is taking place underneath in my spirit.
Amen.

Think Bigger

> "Therefore, I say to all of you, all things for which you pray and ask, believe that you have received them, and they will be granted to you." Mark 11:24

There is a quote I framed on my desk that I found on Instagram. I remember the first time that I saw it, and it struck me like lightning. "Nah, bigger," God. What I used to do growing up is match my dreams to my reality. I would belittle and minimize the dreams put in my heart because I didn't think they were possible. I didn't think it was possible to be able to publish a book so young, let alone write the darn thing. I didn't think it was possible for me to have a chance to play D1 tennis when I was in high school. After seeing that quote, I started challenging my thinking. Why am I matching my dreams to fit my reality? If the God of all the universe is who He says He is, and I am who He says I am, I should be leveling up my reality to fit my dreams.

I started asking God for bigger things. I started praying

bigger prayers. I realized that the doubt I had in myself restrained me from even asking God for the things I really wanted, simply because I didn't think they were possible. Let me remind you- with God, *all* things are possible. Even the biggest, boldest, wildest dreams you could ever possibly have for yourself- are possible. You just have to ask. You have to be bold enough to ask God for that crazy dream you don't think is possible. Then you have to prepare to receive it. When I asked God to give me the strength to write a book and get it published, I started preparing. I started writing. I started organizing and prepping. After every rejection email reply from publishers that said this wasn't the project for them, I kept going. I kept researching. I kept reaching out because I knew my God wouldn't fail me. I know that my God is the God of all things and possibilities, and if it is in His will and His plan for you, He will make it happen. Everything in your life right now is preparing you for the thing you asked God for, make sure you are asking big enough questions. Ask Him what you really want out of life. Are you praying big enough? Are you asking for big enough things? The God that created the entire universe created *you* too. He gave you a heart to dream. Allow yourself to dream bigger. Think bigger.

God, I pray that you give me the strength to dream bigger today. Let myself go there. Let myself think bigger, dream bigger, and not be ashamed to ask for bigger.
Amen.

Stop Pretending

> "Do not let your adorning be external-the braiding of hair and the putting on of gold jewelry, or the clothing you wear-but let your adorning by the hidden person of the heart with the imperishable beauty of a gentle and quiet spirit, which in God's sight is very precious." 1 Peter 3:3-4

We live in an Instagram, Facebook, Twitter, and Tiktok-run world. Social media consumes us everywhere we go. I don't know about you, but sometimes I get so sucked into this vortex of social media that I end up allowing it to define who I am instead of defining myself. I see someone wearing a bikini and looking amazing, and all of a sudden, I feel worse about my body, even though 10 seconds before seeing that photo, I felt fine about it. I see a couple happily married or holding hands, looking at each other with that love in their eyes, and all of a sudden, I start questioning if I am that happy in my own relationship, even though 5 seconds prior to seeing that photo I knew that I absolutely was. Social media is a gateway for comparison. I think, sometimes, it causes us to pretend to be people that we aren't. We take our real life and start showing up to it in the way we would want to show up on social media- edited, filtered, cropped, and perfectly captioned. The thing is, real life doesn't work like that. You cannot edit or filter your reality to make it feel perfect because life isn't perfect. The truth is that you are so busy pretending to be the person you think you need to show on social media, that you are creating a barrier between you and the blessings God wants to give you. God cannot bless the person you pretend to be- He can only bless *you*. The you that He made in His image and designed to do exactly what He needs you to in this world. Stop pretending to be someone you aren't. Stop pretending to be someone that maybe you wish you were right now but know are not. It isn't launching you any further into the purpose that God put you here on this earth for. Realize that the magic and uniqueness that God put in you, yes, even the things that make you "strange" or "weird" or "not Instagramable," are exactly the traits He needed you to have to bless this earth in a specific way. Stop denying them. Stop trying to crop them out of the picture of your life. Accept yourself, in all angles, edits, filters, and forms. You were made for incredible things, my dear, but God cannot bless the person you pretend to be.

God, don't let me miss out on the blessing that you
made me out to be. Help me to stop pretending to be
who I think society wants me to be, and to help me
simply live into the person you made me to be.
Amen.

Siri God

> *"Don't be anxious about anything, but in every situation, by prayer and petition, with thanksgiving, present your requests to God." Philippians 4:6*

I'll be the first to say how much I love Siri. Being the directionally challenged human being that I am, she is my go-to when I need directions somewhere ASAP (which is usually most of the time). No kidding, it took me around four years to get from my school to the chiropractor I see every two weeks without a GPS. Directions are not my strong suit, and it is so nice just to know that I can quickly call on my girl Siri and get everything I need.

The problem with Siri, though, just like everything that comes in big waves with this world of "right now," is that she conditions us to believe we can have everything we want in that same second that we ask for it. I think this then translates into our relationship with God. We expect to pray and receive the answer to our prayer before we even get off our knees. We treat our relationship with God like we do our relationship with Siri- we ask, expect it in less than 5 minutes, and if we don't get what we want, we think that the connection is bad. We think that all of a sudden, it is somehow God's fault or our fault that we aren't getting what we prayed to God for. Listen to me, friend, prayers don't work like that. God isn't a Siri God. God loves you enough to not give you everything that you pray for. He loves you enough to give you what you need, not all that you want. We've got to stop coming to God with the presumption that we can pray for anything, and He'll give it to us that same minute. God wants you to prosper. God wants you to have all the things in your heart that you desire the most. However, God also allows there to be a process that you must go through to get the thing you desire. Steve Harvey once said, "everything you are going through right now is simply preparation to receive the thing you asked God for a while back."

You may have had the energy to ask, but do you have the energy to prepare? Are you willing to go through the process that God is going to take you through to mold you into the person that is mature enough to receive the thing you are asking Him for? God wants you to want a relationship with Him, not just resources from Him. Maybe it's time to ask yourself whether or not you are willing to undergo the process that it takes to become the person available to receive the thing you want most, not what you want most.

God, you are not a Siri God. When I pray to you, help me realize that everything you have in store for me will come in due time. Give me the strength of patience. Help me see that everything worth having comes with massive preparation to receive it.
Amen.

Make It Happen

We hear it all the time- you want something. You've got to go get it. Sometimes, though, it's hard to know whether or not you are capable of going and getting the thing that you set out for. In fact, I would argue that so many of us are afraid we are not capable of the things we deep-down desire, we set our sights low because going for something we know we can achieve and achieving it is much less painful than dreaming for something that you want so much, and not getting it. I want to challenge your thinking for a little bit, though. I used to base all the probabilities on whether or not I could accomplish something on *me*. I didn't realize that the reason God put these huge dreams in my heart wasn't because He believed I could do it, but because He was giving me an opportunity for His strength to work through me. I truly believe that "making it happen" has nothing to do with your ability to make things happen, and everything to do with your willingness to surrender to God working through you. It will lead to discomfort, questions, uncertainty, fear, doubt, and also fulfillment that surpasses your wildest dreams. God wants to work through you. With every dream He places in your heart, it is an invitation He is giving you the opportunity for Him to do just that. The thing is, though, you've got to accept this invitation. Are you going to accept the invitation God is giving you through these huge, big, scary dreams He placed in your heart? Or are you going to shy away and shoot for things that you know you can achieve alone?

Don't give up on who you are because of how things are around you. You may be in a valley right now. You may be at your low. You may be at your peak and experiencing the best that life has yet to offer you in this very minute. Regardless of how things are around you, remember you are still a child of God. He is your number one fan. He wants you to achieve every single thing that He placed in your heart. He wouldn't have put it there if He wasn't planning on providing you the strength you need to fulfill that desire; you must just be willing to let Him in.

God, I surrender. I surrender to all of these dreams you have put in my heart and in my mind. I can see it. I can feel it. I surrender to Your strength and goodness. Let it fill me up to accomplish this dream and pursue it in exactly the way you see.
Amen.

Forget About Your Plan

> "Trust in the Lord with all your heart, and do not lean on your own understanding. In all your ways acknowledge Him, and He will make straight your paths." Proverbs 3:5-6

Where are all my planners out there? The ones that need to know absolutely every detail before acting or deciding on what they want to do. Oh, how I can relate. I used to be someone that was absolutely tormented by a lack of a plan- and in a lot of ways, I still am. Whenever I feel uncertainty is in the mix, I run for the hills. In a way, this helps me get done all the things I know I need to get done, but at the same time, this is one of my greatest setbacks. I think the fear of not having a plan has made me miss out on a lot of things I could've experienced but didn't make myself available too simply because of the fear of what my uncertainty was telling me. Things as little as taking weekend trips that have no itinerary or schedule, freak me out. Some of you may think I am taking things to the extreme, but even those of you that don't live your life by a strict plan, still crave that need for certainty. I know you do. Have you ever struggled with the anxiety of not knowing what you want to do with your life? Feared not knowing that next step you want to take, so you end up making a rash decision on where you think you want to go, but honestly have no idea? Prayed to God, begging for a clear answer on whether or not to accept that job position, get in that relationship, post your resume, have that conversation?

It happens to me a lot. Especially when I have no clue what I want my future to look like. Sometimes it is so clear, and other times, it is just this big fuzzy picture. I am here to tell you, it happens to everyone. I want to remind you, though, that God never promised to give us all the answers. In fact, I think God doesn't want us to know the answers, because if He gave us the blueprints for our life and exactly how it was going to go at the very beginning, there would be no room for faith. Faith looks forward, where we tend to look behind. We look into our past for indications of where we are going in the future, while faith says that every single moment is an opportunity to be born again. You've got to adjust your focus from being concerned so much with *what* your life is, and instead, look at *who* He is that holds your life. You may have no idea where you are going. You may have no plan, but He does. Rest your faith in that.

God, you have a plan for me, so much better than the plan I could ever make for myself. I pray you help me release this grip I have on the plans I think I want for myself and surrender to the goodness you have in store as it comes.
Amen.

The Ultimate Spotter

So, I've been doing this new thing called weightlifting. For the sake of transparency, I don't even know if it's totally fair to call my new exercise regimen that because I am only bearing my body-weight in these workouts, but nonetheless, it is something my cardio loving self is doing to get out of my comfort zone. Going to the "weight" side of the gym was uncharted territory for myself, until three weeks ago, when I got the urge to mix things up a bit. My elliptical, running, stair stepper loving self made the decision to go for it in the weight room. Something I am seeing and learning about is the importance of a good spotter. I don't know how familiar you are with weightlifting, but one of the most important things when you are lifting heavy weight is that you have a spotter watching you while you do it. Now here's the thing about what makes a good spotter, it's all about them being as tuned in as possible to when they need to catch the weight for you if it's too much. It's a hard judgment to make sometimes, simply because you don't want to misjudge and take off the load from the lifter too soon if they are capable of pushing themselves to lift it, but you also don't want to wait too long to help them if they aren't capable of lifting it completely on their own because the lifter could get injured.

God is the ultimate spotter. He doesn't say there won't be heaviness we are going to have to carry throughout our lives, but He would never give us a load to carry on our own that we aren't capable of lifting by ourselves. He is so perfectly in tune with how much weight we can carry and gives us the amount of weight necessary for us to lift to make us stronger, without making us injured. When the load is too heavy to bear, that is when He wants us to turn toward Him, so He can lighten the burden of our backs, just like a spotter does for someone who perhaps overcalculated how much weight they could actually lift. Do not be afraid of heaviness in your heart. If it wasn't intended to make you stronger, God would've lightened the load by now.

God, all the weight on my heart is going to make me stronger. I know this because I have the ultimate spotter. You would never let me crumble under this weight. You know exactly what you're doing with the weight I am bearing. Thank you for having my back.
Amen.

Feel the Pressure

> *"Come to me, all who labor and are heavy laden, and I will give you rest." Matthew 11:28*

Just the other day, I had a mini panic attack simply because there was so much to do, and I actually had no idea how on earth to get it done. Does that ever happen to you? You have a to-do list that seems to never end, and even when you feel like you're making even the slightest progress, all of a sudden, things continue to pile up, and even though you felt ahead two seconds ago, now you feel behind? It's like this never-ending cycle of feeling this pressure to get things done. I feel it all the time. I also get this pressure in my heart where I feel like I have to "perform." Whether it's on social media, speaking, coaching people in the business I am in- I get this feeling of pressure on a consistent basis as if I am not going to show up and perform the way I think I should. All this pressure to be perfect on social media- have the perfect body, the perfect attitude, the perfect filter, the perfect clothing, the perfect hair- it is exhausting.

Here's the thing about pressure, it can be a really informative thing. Pressure comes when something on the inside of us feels like it is coming against something outside of us. Physically, we feel pressure all the time, especially if you work out, you know what I am talking about. To build muscle, you've got to apply pressure to your muscles through weights or resistance bands—the same thing with our spiritual muscles. Pressure does make things harder, but it also makes things stronger if you know how to apply it properly. I think when we feel overwhelmed by the load we are carrying, it can be so destructive, but it can also act as the most amazing reminder that we don't need to carry a cross that Jesus already carried for us. I know when I have thoughts of never being good enough, fears of uncertainty, discomfort in not knowing if I made the right decision or not, it can feel like so much pressure is building up inside of me. That, right there, is always the point when the pressure builds up, that I try to remember God brought Jesus to this world so that I wouldn't have to carry this weight. It's okay if I don't know what to do or don't feel good enough, but it isn't okay for me to bear the load of something that Jesus died to release me from.

Allow the reminder that pressure is simply an indication you are putting too much of the load Jesus came to save you from on yourself.

God, you gave me a Savior to relieve me of all of this pressure. Pressure of perfection, performance, and reputation- You brought Jesus to save me from it all. Help me to see the relief and feel the release of the pressure You have given me.
Amen.

You Don't Have to Carry That

> "But God shows His love for us in that while we were
> still sinners, Christ died for us." Romans 5:8

The other day, I was on the phone with someone very close to me in my life, and they called me incredibly selfish. This stung to the core. The reason I think this stung to the core so much is that part of me was genuinely terrified that I was, in fact, selfish. The reality is? I absolutely am. Sorry to break it to you, if you thought that 69 devotionals into this you were reading the works of a perfect human being, I am absolutely not. I believe Oprah's saying, "your cup must be rennet over," is true. I think to best show up for the people you love in your life and to pour into their cups, you must first have your cup filled. This requires you to have things in your life that are just yours and may not benefit anybody but you at that moment, but help you show up in the best way possible for the people you love later on. The truth is that I struggle regularly with knowing just how much to fill my cup and when to pour into other people. It's never perfect. Sometimes I fill my cup up too much, sometimes I pour what's in my cup out too much. There is no such thing as perfection when it comes to this. Yet when this person told me I was incredibly selfish, for weeks, I felt gutted. I felt so heavy and as if the world of the world was on my shoulders. I felt like a crappy person that didn't deserve to love because I wasn't perfect at it.

In these moments of self-pity and loathing, I realized I was carrying a cross that Jesus had already carried for me. God knew none of us were perfect, that is why He sent Jesus to save us. If we even had the slightest chance of being perfect in this lifetime, there would be no reason for Jesus to need to come to save us. For me, I am way too selfish at times. This is one of my many, many, many faults. For you, you may be quick to anger, rash, blunt, harsh, moody, dishonest, or have any other side to you that you try to conceal. Should we work on those things? Absolutely. However, someone once told me that trying to work on your imperfections, without coming at it from a foundation of self-love, is like building your house on a foundation of sand; it isn't going to last long. You want to work and grow yourself with the understanding that you are beautiful, worthy, valuable, and forgiven. Working on your imperfections through that viewpoint is like building your house of self-improvement on sturdy soil that will support your growth.

God, help me remember that right here, right now, I am forgiven just as I am. All my faults are things to be worked on, but not means to tear down my worth as a human being. You and You alone gave me my worth, so not even my mistakes or the undesirable parts of me can take it away.
Amen.

Who Said Anything About Luck?

> *"Therefore, I tell you, whatever you ask in prayer,*
> *believe that you have received it, and it will be yours."*
> *Mark 11:24*

was having a conversation last night with somebody, and we were talking about successful people. Full disclosure, one of my absolute favorite things to do is study successful people. I love documentaries, biographies, books, podcasts, YouTube videos- anything that talks about how someone of such great success got to where they are. The person I was talking to kept repeating how a lot of it comes down to luck. The people who got to be very successful are simply incredibly *lucky*. This struck something in me there for a second. It didn't sit right. It took me an entire 24 hours, until I am now writing this devotional, to realize why that didn't sit right with me. It's because I don't limit my God to luck. I think luck is a make-believe concept people have created to make themselves feel better as to why they could not be the success someone else is. It gives them a cushion to the blow that somebody else was more established, financially successful, and victorious at something they perhaps once dreamed they would be successful at.

Let me tell you this- it is only the people who gave up on their dreams that would ever try and convince you out of yours. I truly believe that luck comes when preparation meets chance. I think God blesses all of us with these once in a lifetime chances, chances that come by so rare and are so profound it does seem to be plain "luck," but it isn't luck, it's God's blessing to you. However, this goes without saying, I also believe that it is only those that are trusting in this goodness that is bound to come, and preparing to receive it, that actually do something with it. I know a lot of people who have had amazing chances, but because the preparation wasn't there, they never achieved anything. Take most of the people who win the lottery, for example. They had an incredible blessing given to them, but because they were not preparing to receive that blessing by learning the rights of investing, saving, donating, and financially planning, they blew their chance. Luck is not how the most successful people got to where they are now. It is a combination of straight blessings from God, but also preparation on their part amidst their faith that God would provide.

Don't be afraid to ask God for what you want. God wants us to have such great faith in Him that we ask Him for the biggest and grandest of things. Let me ask you this, when you ask your parents for something, is it something that you think they can't provide, or something you know they can provide? Something you know they can provide, exactly. God wants your faith to be so great that you don't put limits on what you ask Him for. Not only do you not put limits on it, but you go ahead and prepare to receive it after you have asked, indicating you know that if God is willing, He is able.

God, I'm done praying small. Help me open up my deepest desires to you. I don't want to be afraid to pray big. You made me fully to rely on you, so here I am. Here is my heart.
Amen.

It's a Process

> *"Delight yourself in the Lord, and He will give you the desires of your heart. Commit your way to the Lord; trust in Him and He will act." Proverbs 3:5-6*

I hate to break it to you like this, my friend, but you cannot tell God how to bless you. Have you ever done that? I know I have so many times. It's so funny, I pray as if I am God's administrative assistant, reminding Him of all the appointments I think He's got with me and that I expect Him to deliver on. I'll pray and be like, "hey, God, remember that thing that I really want so bad, and I haven't gotten yet? Yeah, I just wanted to remind you of that." It's so funny because I think some of us unknowingly really do pray thinking that God is supposed to answer us as if we hold the pen to His calendar, instead of the other way around.

My friends, everything you are going through right now is God preparing you to receive what you asked Him for initially. There is one song that always reminds me of just how powerful it is that God knows better than to answer all of our prayers, and it says, "thank God for unanswered prayers." I know you may not be in a season of life right now where you truly believe God has your best interest at heart, or even hears your prayers. I want to let you know that He does, and your pain is His pain. However, every single ounce of pain you are feeling God will use for good. He will use that pain as part of the process of forming you into the person you need to be to mark this world in the way He needs you to. My old tennis coach used to say all the time, "trust the process," and she was absolutely right. You cannot trust in the everyday ups and downs, but in the larger picture of things, knowing that every single bend in the road to your story is still getting you to that desired destination. You've got to trust that God has your ultimate destination in sight for you, and every setback, disappointment, hurt, and pain is simply part of the journey that it takes to get there.

Trust in Him. Trust in His process.

God, I want to be a true advocate for you and your word, so here I am, surrendering to your process. Use me. Shape me. Mold me. Grow me. Take me on the journey that it means to walk with You through life. Take me through your process.
Amen.

Better is Ahead

> "No dear brothers and sisters, I have not achieved it, but I focus on this one thing: Forgetting the past and looking forward to what lies ahead." Philippians 3:13

This is what I truly believe- faith is the unshakable conviction that what is ahead of you is always better than what is behind. It is the belief that no matter what, the best of things is still in my future and have yet to come to pass. Even on your deathbed, it is recognizing that you are about to enter into all of His glory in Heaven, and the best is yet to come.

I think it is so easy to get into the mindset that our glory days are behind us. The older we get, the more we accomplish and experience, it also seems, the more complicated life gets. This increasing complication and complexity play this trick on you and gets you to start thinking that your best days were behind you when there was less pressure, responsibility, and lower standards for you to reach. I am only 22 years old, and I already understand that the older I get, the more complicated life will be. The more responsibility will be given to me in my life- financially, relationally, physically, mentally, and emotionally. Harder questions must be answered, and greater tests are given. However, I also believe that with this increasing complexity of life, comes a deeper awareness of the gratitude our lives deserve. God gives us everything that we need. God always has our best interest at heart. Trusting in Him is trusting that the further we embark on this journey, the more we continue to have to look forward to. Your glory years, days, and moments are not behind you, they are always in front of you. They may look different than how you initially prayed for them to be, but they will still be the best that has yet to come. The best is always yet to come. When we are in our valley, the best is yet to come. When we cannot see a way out of our circumstance, the best is yet to come. When we have just breathed our last breath, the best is yet to come.

God, I am uncertain of a lot of things, but the one thing I am not uncertain about is that you continue to provide. The best is yet to come. This is my declaration that my faith in you is greater than my fear of the unknown. You are the best. You give me the best. Every day I live is a day closer to receiving the best that is coming my way from you.
Amen.

Put Your Confidence in the Planter

> "Then the Lord formed the man of dust from the ground and breathed into his nostrils the breath of life, and the man became a living creature."
> Genesis 2:7

I truly believe that we all have seeds of greatness that lie within us. The Bible says that each of us was made and crafted from the dirt of the earth. I heard Pastor Robert Madu explain that the reason for this is because seeds can grow in dirt. God has placed a seed of greatness in each and every one of our hearts. Every single person's seed looks different. Some of you are called to be an incredible speaker, some poets, some doctors, teachers, lawyers, and others are called to be moms or dads. We are all called to be different things and many things at the same time. God put in our heart's little seeds of greatness, but we are responsible for watering those seeds. He gave us the seed; we must grow it.

Never let anyone tell you how far you can go in life. They do not know what you are capable of growing into. How do I know this? They did not plant your seed. They have no idea what you are capable of because they did not make you, God did. So before you let anyone tell you how far you can go, what you can accomplish, or what you are capable of doing with your life, remember, it isn't the people in this world that crafted you and put your seed of greatness in your heart, but the Creator. Let your confidence lie in Him that you can do all the things He set in your heart for you to do. Every day, wake up with the intention to water that seed of greatness He put in your heart. Too many times, I see people sleepwalking through their potential. They let other people determine how far they are going to go, or they just go through life, intentionally unaware of the greatness inside of them. The God that made the universe, handcrafted you. Not only that, but He put a seed of greatness in you that He intends you to water every single day so it can grow into the magnificence that is your purpose. Don't waste that. Don't give the world the disservice that is you not living to your potential. The world needs your greatness. The world needs you to water your seed so you can grow into the blossom you were intended to be to light up this world.

God, you gave me a seed of greatness. Even if I don't even know what that seed is intended for yet, help me to water it every single day by keeping my focus on you. I am here for a reason. You sent me here with a purpose. I pray you give me the strength and the courage to live it out in a world that tries to tell me who I get to be.
Amen.

It's Okay, Not to Be Okay

> "For the Lord is good; His loving kindness is everlasting and His faithfulness to all generations."
> Psalm 100:5

I used to think I had to be happy all the time. I thought getting sad or upset was a bad thing and made me a bad person. Growing up, I was always referred to as the "happy girl," which I took pride in because I felt like my gift was to make other people happy. The problem with this thinking, or one of the dozen I should say, is that when I was upset about something, I would suppress my emotions because if I was upset, I couldn't make the people around me happy. What this led to, despite the delusion that I was in control for others' happiness instead of themselves, was a young girl that was falling apart at the seams because I had all of these emotions I would never let out. I felt like it was a bad thing not to be happy. I felt that it wasn't okay to not be okay.

God is good. God is so good. God is so good all the time, and guess what? You're not God, neither am I. It is okay for you not to be good all the time. It doesn't mean you're a bad person or a bad Christian. It doesn't mean you don't believe that the Lord is good all the time and has You in His hand always. What it does mean is that you are human, and you have human emotions just like the rest of us. Only God, as far as I am concerned, is good all the time, because He's God. Understanding that God doesn't ask us to be okay all the time is so important. In fact, Jesus even said that the Savior came for the broken, just as a doctor is needed by the sick. When we are broken, upset, and confused, we must look to Him. If we don't embrace our emotions and try to bottle them all up like I did when I was little, that is when a situation that we could have' relied on God for, now becomes suppressed because we didn't offer up to Him all the sadness, hurt, and pain we are feeling. God wants your pain. God wants your sorrow. Yes, God is good all the time, but that doesn't mean you are supposed to be too. We are living a human experience, that includes emotions and circumstances that are not always sunshine and rainbows. It is okay not to be okay.

God, I offer up to you all of my pain today. Every little ounce of sadness, grief, depression, guilt, shame, and anger that lies in me at this moment and future moments, I give it to you. I want you a part of what I am feeling. Here I am.
Amen.

Chase Purpose, Not Popularity

> "For what does it profit a man if he gains the whole world and loses or forfeits himself?" Luke 9:25

Here's the thing no one tells you when you're young: living your purpose, and being the most popular are very different things. We were all given a purpose on this earth; I truly believe that. I think everyone's purpose is to serve one another through love, but how you serve the people in this world depends on your passion. We all have the same purpose, yes, but very different passions. Some people are passionate about being a lawyer, other teachers, some doctors or writers, and other entrepreneurs. How you were made to serve this world is entirely up to the gift God put in you and your decision to follow it or not. When I was younger, I used to think following your passion and purpose was such an easy road. I was fortunate to have parents that told me I could be whatever I wanted to be, so I right from the start, I was cultivated into a dreamer mentality. I dreamed every day about all the things I could do and who I could be. I wanted to be a Disney princess at first, then a singer, then a songwriter, and now I want to be a professional motivational speaker. Isn't it beautiful? The bliss of dreaming about who you can be.

The thing is that now I actually have more clarity about who I was made to be and my purpose here on this earth than I did when I was ten and was wishing to be an animated Disney character. I feel with every ounce of my being that I was made to speak, write, and pour into other people with the good news of God. Living for this purpose, however, has its costs, and if you decide to live for your purpose, you will also go through these costs. The cost of losing people that don't want you to be what you want to be, but what they want you to be. The cost of constantly asking yourself if you're good enough. The cost of never knowing if you'll actually achieve the things God put in your heart. When you start living as who God created you to be, if anything, you will get less popular than ever. Why? Because the enemy tries to prevent us as much as possible from living with our God-given gifts. A lot of times, to prevent you from tapping into all of your potential, the enemy will use people to tell you what you can and cannot do.

The world will try and tell you who you are, don't let them. You've got to define yourself and your purpose to the world before it does it for you.

God, you gave me a purpose here on this earth. Give me the strength to chase your purpose for me over popularity. Faith over fans. Faith over followers.
Amen.

The Price of Admission

When I was younger, I used to think life was so simple. You can be anything your heart desires. You dream of becoming something, work your butt off until you get it, and then live happily ever after. At first, I wanted to be a Disney princess, then an officer in the Air Force, then a priest, then a teacher, and now I want to be a writer and a speaker. What people never tell you, though, is that all the incredibly successful people that have lived into the greatness God called their life to provide had the same price to pay. They all have to pay the price of other people thinking they are crazy.

The world doesn't like uncertainty. The world doesn't like different. The world doesn't like things it cannot control, and the calling God has placed in your heart is just that. Your calling is unlike anyone else's, and because of that, it is also something the world could not possibly be familiar with because it is something it has never seen before. We live in a society that likes to tell you who you are, how far you can go, what you are capable of, and who you can be. God says that you can be all things He has called you to be. The moment you start living with the gift God gave you and the dreams He has set for you, the world is going to start resisting. You will feel tension, and you will probably question what the heck you are doing in the first place. Let that be your first indication that you are moving in the right direction. When the world thinks you're crazy and projects onto you their uncertainty about your future, yet you feel more certain than ever you are moving in the direction God has planned for you, that is when you know you are on to something. The truth is that to make your mark in this world in the way God has planned for you, you're going to experience resistance. You're going to experience hate. You're going to experience people who think they know what's best for you, people who disagree with you, people who used to be your closest friends that now no longer want to speak to you. This doesn't make you a bad person; this makes you someone living for their purpose. As long as you walk the path God has made for you with love, kindness, and the character that Jesus embodied as He walked through His purpose on this earth with all the resistance from people it entailed, you are doing exactly what you need to be doing.

Don't be fooled into thinking that you can live with purpose simultaneously with living for popularity. The price of admission into greatness is giving up pleasing everyone. To live your purpose, you cannot live your life to please other people, but instead, to live for the God that gave you your purpose in the first place.

God, help me keep my eyes on you. It is when my eyes start looking around me instead of up at you that I start to question whether or not I have what it takes to live into this purpose you gave me. I am enough because you made me enough. Not everyone will see that, but You do, and that is what matters.
Amen.

Broken Mirror Mentality

> "And I am convinced that nothing can ever separate
> us from God's love. Neither death nor life, neither
> angels nor demons, neither our fears for today nor
> our worries about tomorrow—not even the powers of
> hell can separate us from God's love. No power in the
> sky above or in the earth below—indeed, nothing in
> all creation will ever be able to separate us from the
> love of God that is revealed in Christ Jesus our Lord."
> Romans 8:38-39

There is an old adage that talks about a woman who was looking into a broken mirror. The mirror had been shattered, so the woman's reflection was crooked, twisted, and broken up, just like the glass in the mirror. The woman, seeing that her image was all broken up, immediately thought that what the mirror showed was the truth of what she looked like, and that meant something was wrong with her. She started to call herself ugly, broken, crooked, and hideous. She took the broken image the broken mirror showed her to be proof that she herself was broken.

Sounds kind of ridiculous, right? Of course, we say that it is common sense to know that when looking into a broken mirror and our reflection is broken and crooked, it is because the mirror is shattered, not because we actually look like that. However, why is it that when we look at a broken world to tell us our worth and value, and it comes back to tell us that we are no more than a broken image, we take it as truth? We look to this world for so many answers as to who we are, why we are here, what our purpose is, and what our worth is. If you look at something broken for answers, your answers are always going to be broken too. I want to remind you that God made you beautiful and in His image, not in the world's image. Every single part of you, from your freckles to your nose, hair, birthmark, skin tone, body type, the way you speak, and so on, was designed perfectly by Him just for you. Stop looking at the world to tell you your worth. You are worthy not because the world says so, but because God made you worthy before the world even knew who you were.

The world says that you are broken, God says that you are His beautiful masterpiece in progress. The world says you're "too much," God says you are exactly enough. The world says you are too fat, too ugly, your nose is too big, your hair is too dark, your skin is too pale, but God says you are the only version of you that He has have ever created in the entire history of mankind. The world will say you are a failure, God says failure for you is impossible because you've already received the greatest victory of all- His unconditional love.

God, you made me, me for a reason. You gave me all these incredible gifts for a purpose. Help me define myself and my worth by the reflection You show me, and not the broken reflection the world portrays to me. Amen.

You've Got to Trust

> "But blessed is the one who trusts in the Lord, whose confidence is in Him. They will be like a tree planted by the water that sends out its roots by the stream. It does not fear when heat comes; its leaves are always green. It has no worries in a year of drought and never fails to bear fruit." Jeremiah 17:7-8

I used to think that if I wasn't successful at something, I wasn't trying hard enough. The problem with that logic is that no matter how hard I tried or what all I was doing, if I hadn't been successful yet, then it was proof that I was somehow insufficient as a person. I remember the first year at Wofford on the tennis team when I didn't make the lineup, I was crushed. Shattered would even be a fair word for it if I am being honest. I was putting in all the extra hours, watching the film outside of practice, and doing all the things that my coach said I needed to do to claim a spot in the starting lineup- and it still didn't happen. In fact, it never did. I was trying so hard, and because my entire life I had been told that if you try hard enough, you'll eventually succeed, I was left so confused. There was no way I could possibly try any harder than I already had.

That's the thing about faith- it isn't about how hard you try, but how hard you trust. God doesn't ask us to try and succeed with Him because He already knows that our trying will always be inadequate. That is why He extends His hand out to us and does the heavy lifting for us. All you are asked to do is extend your hand in trust to reach His. That freshman year of college, what I didn't realize was that all my trying was preventing me from doing the one thing God needed me to do the most, which was to trust His process and His timing. It was only when I surrendered to trusting His plan, instead of trying to make my plan work, that I ended up in a place I was truly happy.

God doesn't ask you to try your way to victory because He has already given you victory. All He asks is that you trust in the path He has already paved for you and surrender to His will.

God, I surrender. I pray that I stop trying so fervently to make my plan work and instead just trust in yours. Help me show up to trust.
Amen.

Weariness is not Weakness

> "Come to me, all you who are weary and burdened, and I will give you rest." Matthew 11:28-30

Sometimes, I just feel like it's all too much, like the more I work toward something, the more behind I become. Have you ever felt like that? It's like no matter how hard you try, how much effort you put in, or how much ground you think you are covering, the list of things you haven't done seems to continue to grow when you aren't looking. The other day, I remember, just thinking, 'I am so tired.' It's almost like we live in a world where we aren't supposed to be tired. We are somehow supposed to be the person who can show up to work after crushing a workout, eating a stellar breakfast, crushing our job, taking care of the kids, having amazing relationships, making a good income, volunteering for all the committees, and still having time to grow ourselves personally. If we admit we're tired, we've somehow failed by society's standards.

I want to remind you (and myself), it's okay to get tired. We have a God that will fight with us, stand up for us, love us, battle with us, but will also rest with us. Jesus has even said before that He was tired after a long journey. I think we need to stop looking at being tired as a sign of weakness, and instead, understand it is a sign of our humanity. It is a sign that we are in need of something bigger than us to fuel us. We are in need of God. Our weariness is the exact thing that pinpoints us back to our Heavenly Father. Imagine if we never got tired, we never felt defeated, or we never felt weary? We would think we could do all things all the time. We would never look to our Heavenly Father for fuel. We would never look to the bread of life to replenish us.

We were not made to do everything and do it all perfectly. We are human, not superhuman. We can have days when we aren't feeling up to everything. We can have moments where we admit that we may have pushed ourselves too far than we could handle. We can have a time where we realize we may need to pump the brakes instead of flooring the gas pedal in our lives for once. All animals have seasons of hibernation or rest. Why do we humans think that rest is such a bad thing? God loves us because we are human. We are imperfect, meaning we were not made to wear all the hats. It's okay to say you are tired, in fact, it's okay to be tired. It doesn't mean you are weak; it may just mean that you are in a season where you need to reset and reboot.

God, help remind me that taking a break is okay. You did not design me to go 100% all of the time. Help me look to you for both my fuel in my "go" seasons and my recovery in my off seasons.
Amen.

What Would Your Answer Be?

> "Therefore, if anyone is in Christ, he is a new creation.
> The old has passed away; behold, the new has come."
> 2 Corinthians 5:17

I was walking with my brother on the beach today, and I asked him a question I think we should all ask ourselves from time to time. I asked him if he were to die tomorrow (sorry if that is a little too dark for you in your morning), what would his biggest regret be as of right now? I also asked him what thing is he the proudest of in his life at this very moment.

Sometimes, I think we get so focused on looking ahead and how much further in life we have to go, that we forget to look behind us. I feel like in today's world, "looking behind" has gotten such a bad rep. It is as if all the emphasis is on looking forward and only looking forward, but I don't think that should be the case all the time. If you don't take the time to look back at how far you have come, all you have accomplished, learn from the mistakes you've made, you may be pressing forward, yes, but what progress will be made? God gave us life to not only look forward but also to learn from. One of the best people you can learn from is yourself. Look behind you and reflect on your life. Think about the person you were a year ago- would they be proud of the person you are today? Would they be *inspired* by the person you are today? If not, that's the beauty of the future; you can always strive to become better and stronger. However, sometimes you don't know what better and stronger means to you until you take the time to look back at your past and identify where you are bouncing off from. Ask yourself the hard questions- for your life up to this point, what is the biggest regret you have? What is the proudest moment or accomplishment you have? Don't be afraid to celebrate yourself for the good things, and also dive deep into the painful. Sometimes we keep the past because the mistakes that make it up are so painful, we avoid it as much as we can, at all costs. I encourage you, do not be afraid of your past. It is, in fact, confronting your past and understanding God creates every day as an opportunity to rise again and live your life in honor of Him, that you release the chains of the past from having any grip on you.

God, I am not my past, I am who you say I am. That is why I have nothing to lose by looking back and seeing the ways I can grow. Thank you for making my new every day that I rise again.
Amen.

Don't Try It Alone

> *"For the sake of His great name the Lord will not reject His people, because the Lord was pleased to make you His own."* 1 Samuel 12:22

There's a pretty popular myth that I think a lot of people fall prey to believing; that you can do life alone. Now yes, I will say that people take this myth to different extremes; not everyone goes into full isolation mode and refuses to let anyone into their lives. However, I think a lot of people have certain places in their lives they prevent people from seeing. For some people, it is their work or their business, for some, it's their emotions, and for others, it's a certain character trait they are so afraid of showing to other people, they hide it from everyone they care about. For most people, they have some part of their lives they are hesitant to show other people. I know, for me, for the longest time, it was the parts of me that weren't happy. I felt like my job was to make everyone else happy, and in doing so, I could never be upset myself. Now it isn't humanly possible to be happy 100% of the time, so what I would do is hide my tears from everyone I knew. I didn't want anyone to see me upset. I thought I could handle my pain, hurt, and tears all by myself.

God didn't craft us to handle life by ourselves. He didn't make us to handle pain, hurt, torment, obstacles, challenges, fear, or any emotion similar to that alone. One of the most beautiful blessings God has given us is the blessing to go through life with other people. To fully heal, one must expose that wound. I am not saying expose your wound to just any and everyone, sometimes that can make the wound cut even deeper. However, I am saying that with the right people sharing what is hurting you is part of the healing process. People have been around for a long time. I guarantee, whatever it is you are going through, someone has already been through it. Now, because we are all individuals, they will be feeling the exact same things as you are. However, if they can listen or relate in some way, it provides healing in a way you never thought possible.

God gave us Him, and each other, to go through life with. We were not made to go through life alone. If you think it would just be easier to go through life alone, trust me when I say that is your ego talking. In the long term, there is so much more pain experienced when you isolate yourself from people who want to love and help you. If you are in a place where you feel like no one in your corner wants to do that, know that your Heavenly Father made you to depend on Him to heal your pain. However, to do that, you must show and expose it to Him.

God, I show you my pains. I do not want to go through this life alone, especially without you. Here is my heart Lord, shine your light to heal my wounds.

Dear, Little Voices

> "My sheep hear my voice, and I know them, and they follow me. I give them eternal life, and they will never perish, and no one will snatch them out of my hand."
> John 10: 27-28

When I was younger and would get nervous before a tennis match, my dad would tell me that it was okay to be nervous. He would say that once I got out there and started playing, I would start to loosen up. For a while, that is what, in fact, happened, but then when I went through the college recruiting process and coaches started to watch me play, something changed. I started to get more nervous as the match went on. I would get so nervous that I couldn't even hit the tennis ball because I could already see the ball going out or in the net before I'd even hit it. I would freeze up so much that I hated being out there at all. It's like the more pressure I felt, the more I froze. I just couldn't tune it out as everyone told me to because these little voices in my head would constantly tell me I wasn't good enough. I would be on the baseline ready to serve, and the little voice would tell me it was going to go out, or that I was going to double fault. I'd be at the net waiting for the ball to land in that sweet spot on my racket for an overhead winner, but the little voices would tell me right before I hit it that I was going to shank it.

You probably have little voices too. Little voices telling you you're not this or that. They're telling you you're not good enough, smart enough, a loser, a failure, not pretty enough, or not accomplished enough. They may tell you that you're not worth forgiving, that you are a horrible person, or that you are a waste of space. I say this because these little voices in my head have told me that at one time or another as well. The truth? There is no way of getting rid of them. What you can do, though, is realize there is another voice inside you- the voice of God. These little voices cannot be destroyed, but they can be weakened when you choose to listen to the voice in you that tells you that you are a child of God, strong, beautiful, worthy, valuable, already forgiven, and capable of doing all things with Christ's strength in you. The voice you listen to is the voice you follow. Choose to make that voice, the voice of truth, louder than the voice that is crippling you.

God, help me make these little voices quieter than the voice of your truth in me. You called me your child, so your truth is what I want to live into and define my life by
Amen.

Be the Best You, Not the Best Them

> "For we are his workmanship, created in Christ Jesus for good works, which God prepared beforehand, that we should walk in them." Ephesians 2:10

Did you grow up having people you looked up to? I sure hope so! I grew up wanting to be Selena Gomez on *Wizards of Waverly Place* for a short amount of time, then I was inspired by Hermione Granger as I got on my Harry Potter kick, and then it led to my inspiration of the infamous Oprah Winfrey. I have had so many women that have inspired me in so many ways. Something that I didn't realize until recently, though, is that I took this inspiration a step too far; I wanted to *be* these women. I wanted to become the next Oprah Winfrey, Rachel Hollis, and Lysa Terkuesrt. I wasn't just inspired by them, but I changed myself in a way to make it so I could look more like them, dress like them, and talk like them. I remember, I even cut my hair to look like Hermione's in the third *Harry Potter*!

What I realize now, but did not realize growing up, was that it is healthy to be inspired by other people, but inspiration and imitation are two very different things that share a very fine line. When we are inspired by others in a healthy way, we let that inspiration fuel us showing up and growing into the best version of ourselves. When we are inspired by others in an unhealthy way, we aren't using the attributes we admire of them to become a better version of *us*, but instead, try to become another version of them.

It is such a beautiful thing to be inspired by people, but I challenge you to recognize when you are using that inspiration in a healthy way versus an unhealthy way. Use that inspiration as fuel to level up to the best version of yourself. You don't want to be another version of that person you are inspired by; you want to be the best and first version of *you* in this world; the version that God created you to be.

God, you made me for a reason. Help me become inspired by other people but live into the one of a kind version that is me. Help me be the first and best me. Amen.

Doubt is a Good Thing

> "Trust in the Lord with all your heart, and do not lean on your own understanding. In all your ways acknowledge him, and he will make straight your paths. Be not wise in your own eyes; fear the Lord and turn away from evil. It will be healing to your flesh and refreshment to your bones." Proverbs 3:5-8

feel like we live in a world where it is a bad thing to be doubtful. It's like if you don't believe in something 2,000%, it's the equivalent of you not believing it at all. I think a lot of faith followers believe this to an extent. They think that if they have any doubts whatsoever about God, Jesus, or their faith, they have somehow sinned or are feeling something wrong. I want to be the first to tell you (in case you haven't already been enlightened) that doubt is a beautiful thing. It is the first gift of mystery that Heaven gives us. If we didn't have doubt, there would be no reason for faith to exist. Think about it. If we all knew as fact the good news of the Bible and the reality of Heaven, there would be no room for faith because we would already have the answers. In the dictionary, faith is defined as a strong conviction based on apprehension rather than proof. Faith, in itself, is the very thing we are called to have. Not proof. Not 100% certainty. Not "without a doubt." Not evidence. God wants us to have faith in Him, even when we cannot see it and have no tangible proof.

Doubt is such a beautiful thing, my friends. Doubt is not the absence of faith but is, in fact, the means to obtain it. To reach a point where you have faith in something, you must first start in a place where you are extremely doubtful, or unaware of what it is that you believe exactly. Faith thrives in the very essence of doubt. It is the greatest oxymoron of our time. It is certainty in the uncertainty. It is confidence in the lack of confidence. It is peace in the unknown. It is understanding that you don't need to know and prove everything to believe in the one thing that matters. Doubt is the steppingstone for faith. All the questions that I know you have going on in your head and that you're afraid to ask sometimes. God isn't afraid of them. You can ask them. In fact, I encourage you to ask them, because it is in our questions that your greatest opportunities for growth lie. You may not understand everything, but just as the scripture above says, we were not called to lean on our own understanding. God knows, and He understands. We are simply called to lean in and follow.

God, You aren't afraid of my questions. You aren't afraid of my doubts. Help me to not be either.
Amen.

Faith in the Middle

There are some days I just don't feel like I am getting anywhere. Have you ever had that feeling? It's like I feel so far away from the mesmerizing place called "there." I always want to be "there;" whether there is home, while I am sitting in traffic, the point where all the things I dream of come true, the moment when the person I am mad at apologizes to me, the second this devotional is published, or the season in my life where I feel like I am living fully into my purpose. We all have that "there," or that place that we wish we were at instead of wherever we are currently. It can get so easy to just miss all the blessings we currently have in our life, by looking forward to the place we want to be instead. The thing is, though, we don't have a "their" God or a "someday" God, we have a right now God. We have a God that doesn't care if we are at our financial goals yet,

He loves us now. He doesn't care if we have landed that speaking role, job position, promotion, had that baby, or achieved that next thing we want to achieve yet, He loves us throughout our entire journey. The question isn't whether or not God is with you in the middle of your journey, but whether or not you will keep the faith in the middle. It is really easy to keep faith when you are just starting out on your journey of life before things get tough. It's also easy to keep the faith when you have finally arrived to wherever "there" is in your mind. What is hard is to keep praising, worshiping, and crying out to God when we feel like He has abandoned us. When we feel like there is nothing going our way, and we are never going to get to "there."

Please hear me when I say, your "there" isn't nearly as good as God's. So, when you feel as if the path of your life at this current moment isn't going according to your plans of how you should get "there," it's because it probably isn't! God is taking you somewhere that is so much better, but you've got to have faith in the middle to continue to the place He has for you in the end.

God, help me have faith in the middle. Whatever comes my way, however discouraged I feel, I pray that I find strength in You and Your unfailing love.

You Have Not, Because You Ask Not

> *"Therefore, I tell you, whatever you ask in prayer, believe that you have received it, and it will be yours."*
> *Mark 11:24*

The biggest changes started happening in my life when I started asking God for what I wanted. Steve Harvey gave me this advice (not personally but through one of his many YouTube motivational videos), and ever since I heard it, I started constantly asking God for what I wanted. Now, I know what you're probably thinking, "God isn't a slot machine God, you can't just expect to ask for what you want, pull the trigger, and then it's right there," and I completely agree. What I do believe, though, is the power of letting God know that you truly believe He is capable of giving you all that you desire. You have not because you ask not. Stop praying small. I know you think you've got to pray these small, little prayers, but did you know that we serve an enormous, big, huge God? A God that can make any one of your wishes come true with just the slightest bit of His favor?

I think people pray too small. I also think that faith is the point where you realize He is capable, but not always willing. I understand that when I ask God for things, He is capable of making whatever I asked Him for come to pass, but whether or not He is willing is something that I have no control over. He wants what is best for me; that I know. What I don't know sometimes is if what I want for myself is best for me. That is why I ask God for it. If I keep asking God for it, and it comes true, I know that not only did God allow this thing to come to pass in my life because I asked, but I have assurance it is in His will for my life as well, or else it never would've happened. If I ask God for something and it does not come into my life, I know it was never part of His plan for me, and there are so many better things ahead.

Don't be afraid to dream bigger. Think bigger. Pray bigger. Ask bigger. Asking God for bigger things has nothing to do with your ego or greed, but instead, it is a testimony to what you truly believe HE is capable of. Start asking and ask BIG.

God, I give to you my hopes. I give to you my dreams. I am not afraid to start asking for what I want, and I mean what I truly want. Help me ask bigger. Think bigger. Dream bigger. With you, all things are possible, and all my asks are a testimony to my belief in that. Amen.

How Do You Talk To God?

> "The Lord is near to all who call on him, to all who
> call on him in truth. He fulfills the desire of those who
> fear him; he also hears their cry and saves them."
> Psalm 145: 18-19

I still remember how I talked to God when I was little. I talked to Him like I would the preacher that was standing in the front of my church every Sunday; always using "Yessir," "No sir," "Please sir," as my totally Southern nature kicked in. I used to be so uptight when I was talking to God. I felt like I couldn't say anything wrong, or else I would be punished, or something bad would happen. I think a lot of people feel like that, and that's why they just don't talk to God.

Once I realized that God wants to hear all things I have to say, as if He is my best friend, things started to change. My relationship with Him deepened. I realized that every single little thing I was so afraid to tell God in fear of "getting in trouble," He already knew, and He loved me anyway.

Now I talk to God without even thinking about it. I talk to Him in the shower, in the car, on the way to the gym, during the day making my PB toast, and even on my runs. It feels so good to have the kind of relationship with Him where I know I can tell Him anything, and I know He wants me to tell Him everything.

That's the beauty of grace. I am not ashamed to come to God with my horrible, embarrassing, greedy, sinful thoughts because I know He is not surprised by them. In fact, it is in expressing them to God that I feel more control over not giving in to them, than if I didn't express them to Him. That is the beauty of grace. The beauty of mercy. The beauty of His love. He loves all of us, not just the good parts. Don't be afraid to talk to Him about all the things on your heart- the real things. It's really easy to talk to Him about all the things you are grateful for and thank Him for your blessings, but don't be afraid to talk about the pain you are going through right now. Don't be afraid to mention that hurt you experienced when something you wanted to happen, didn't. He made you to have conversations with Him and to include Him in this life He gave you to live. Include Him in all parts of it.

God, I want to have the courage to bring you everything-
the good, the bad, the pretty and the ugly. I know you love
all parts of me, so I pray that I include you into this life
you gave me. Even when I am embarrassed, or it would be
so much easier to not say anything, I pray that I let you in.
Amen.

One Step at a Time

Sometimes I feel like I am going so fast and doing so much, but not making any sort of real progress. It's like I am on a treadmill. I think I am going fast, yet I am not really getting anywhere. Have you ever felt like that?

Someone once said that you should be cautious of becoming the equivalent of an octopus on rollerblades; lots of motion going on but there is no real progress moving forward in one direction. I think, we as humans, push ourselves to the brink when it comes to being "busy" and doing as much as we humanely can throughout our day. It's almost as if being busy has become a badge of honor in our society. We think that being busy is the equivalent to being important, needed, or valuable. The problem is that

I think too many people are becoming busier and busier with the wrong stuff. Remember that your busy work is not your life's work. You don't want to get to the end of your life having climbed the ladder and realize you climbed the wrong ladder.

Now I know you're probably wondering, what the heck does life's work mean? I am referring to your dreams. Yes, that thing that God put in your heart so that every time you think about it, you get excited. Whether it be to sing, write, build, dance, speak, or serve; make sure that in all the craziness of your life, you are actually moving forward and making progress in the work that is your life's work. Doing just one thing a day, whether that be visualizing, writing down your goals, communicating with others your plans, or working toward your plans, can make all the difference from you being some who is "busy" but making no progress, and someone who is getting things done intentionally.

God, you gave me my dreams for a reason. Help me take things one step at a time, and consistently have more intention as to where I am going with each of the dreams you have given me.
Amen.

Why Is It Taking So Long?

➤

> *"For I know the plans I have for you,"* declares the
> LORD, *"plans to prosper you and not to harm you,*
> *plans to give you hope and a future." Jeremiah 29:11*

You want to know what is really frustrating? And I mean *really* frustrating? When you have a dream, you can feel it with every fiber of your being, you continue to water that seed of the dream day in and day out, and there is still nothing to show for it. I feel this way legitimately every single day, at least once. Now let me be really clear- there's a difference between the frustration you experience when you have actually done the work every single day that you feel called to water the seed God planted in your heart, and the frustration after not having done anything to move forward toward your goals. One is called for; one is not so called for. Sometimes it just feels absolutely depleting. Getting up every single day, doing the work, reaching for the goals I want to hit, and at the end of the day, sometimes there is still nothing to show for it, or so it seems.

Every single season where I have felt this way, some season down the road, I realized that the things God was teaching me in the waiting, allowed me to reach the success I did later on. The reason success takes a long time is because not everyone is willing to go through the process that is necessary to obtain it. If achieving success, purpose, and fulfillment was easy, everyone would have done it, and our world would be so much different. Are you going to be one of the few that stays in for the long haul? Are you going to be one of the rare people that waters the seed of their dream every single day without fail? Even when it is hard, confusing, upsetting, painful, gut-wrenching, and discouraging? It's totally up to you. God loves us enough to place a seed of greatness in our hearts, are you going to decide to continue to water it for however long it takes until it starts sprouting?

God, thank you for the seed of greatness you put on my heart, specifically crafted just for me. I pray that I continue to water this seed, day in and day out, no matter what storms come my way
Amen.

Don't Miss It

> "The Lord will keep your going out and your coming
> in from this time forth and forevermore."
> Psalm 121:8

Sometimes I think I am moving at such a fast pace that I forget to stop, look, and take in everything around me. It's like I am so dead set on getting to a destination, I forget to enjoy the journey to get there. I remember, ever since I was little, I was the kid that would ask, "are we there yet?" I could never seem to enjoy the "getting there" or the process of getting to our destination. I wanted to be there already.

I realized recently, I do this in almost every aspect of my life. Even with my writing, I just want things to be done. There is nothing that frustrates me more than the elongated process of editing, revising, and then re-revising, because I just want it to be done. Yes, you probably just read that and started questioning why the heck you were reading this devotional then, but I think this is something we are all guilty of- especially in the things we care about the most. I care about you all getting to read this devotional because I know it'll change lives. That is why I am so impatient about the long process before the moment it can hit the market. The thing is, God is not just a destination-God, He is a God of the journey too. Sometimes, we can get so fixated on where we want to be and where we think we are headed, we miss out on the very thing that God has called us to realize in the very moment we are in. Don't miss out on the blessings God is giving you right now, but you are so focused on what you don't have that you don't see it.

God, thank you for everything you have given me. The things I do notice and the countless blessings you give me that I do not. I pray you give me the strength to start recognizing the beautiful aspects of the journey and understand the journey is just as important in the process as the destination because that is where who I am is formed.
Amen.

Take a Breath

> "But you are a chosen people, a royal priesthood, a
> holy nation, God's special possession, that you may
> declare the praises of him who called you out of
> darkness into his wonderful light." 1 Peter 2:9

So, I learned something this morning. The reason Yahweh was given the name "Yahweh" is because ancient Hebrew leaders felt that every time they breathed, it sounded like "Yahweh." This made it so every time you took a breath, that breath was blessed, and God was with you. Isn't that amazing? Think about it for a second. How peaceful would our lives be if we lived this thought that with every breath we took, God was blessing us. That is the truth, my friends. Every breath you take is an indication that you are still here, living, breathing, and sent for a purpose God has for you. If you are not dead, you are not done. This line is in an Elevation Worship song, and it couldn't be more spot on. I used to think that I was a waste of space. Sometimes I would get so down with myself that I would feel that there was no point for my life, as if I was as good as dead because my life didn't matter. I am here to tell you that if you are reading this page right now, your life matters. God is using you for something. Do I know what exactly? No. However, I have full confidence that the God that created the universe and you and me and the animals, is an intentional God, and He doesn't just give life to anyone. He gives it to those He intends to use. Maybe this entire time, He was just waiting for you to get to the point where you stood up from your fear, belittlement, anger, suppression, and looked up to Him to say, "use me." He wants you to know that He's got you. He wants you to know that with every breath you take, you still have a purpose here on this Earth that He designed you to fulfill.

God, you brought me into this world, and now I need you to give me the strength to stay in it and follow into my purpose you have for me in it.
Amen.

Don't Go There

> "But I say to you who hear, Love your enemies, do good to those who hate you," Luke 6:27

Have you ever been "irked" by someone? I mean the kind of irk that you just don't understand why they are the way that they are? Yeah, I have been there. It is so funny how the same mouth that can sing gospel music at church on Sunday can also say some words toward someone that I won't repeat in this devotional because it doesn't go with the whole "devotional" theme. I'm sorry if up until this point, you thought that I was this perfect, pure, and innocent person that never said nor thought a cuss word or had any sort of distaste for someone in her life because if that is the case, you are seriously mistaken.

Sometimes people just get under my skin! Anyone out there feel me? It's like why you have to be so competitive. So snobby? So, know-it-all?

The thing is, and this is the biggest thing, *they* are

also God's child. Now I will tell you right off the bat that treating them as my sister or fellow child of God is not my first reaction after they do something that just irks me, so to speak. However, what I want to remind you is that it is okay to be irritated by people. It is okay to be upset, angry at, annoyed with, and maybe even totally despise people, but just don't stay there. Don't stay in that low place of anger and resentment. Don't stay in that place of tormented bitterness. Don't stay in that place of envy, jealousy, or contempt, because that's where evil wins. Evil doesn't win in our initial reaction, but it wins in the long-term captivity of bitterness. Bless and release, my friends. When you are frustrated, upset, angry, and straight-up pissed (yes, I cussed in a devotional book), feel all of your pain, but don't you dare stay there. After a while, get up, started walking, and release the person that is giving you such contempt.

God, you made me out of love. Help me walk this earth in it. Help me understand that I am your child, but so is every single other person. I know that I won't always be able to radiate love, forgiveness, and kindness, but when I am filled with anger or bitterness, give me the strength to get up from that pit. Amen.

Who Are You?

> "Before I formed you in the womb, I knew you, and before you were born, I consecrated you; I appointed you a prophet to the nations." Jeremiah 1:5

Who you are, is not what you do, my friends. I am going to keep this one short and sweet. Isn't it so funny how whenever someone introduces you, they usually follow the initial "this is so and so" introduction with what you *do*? In college, this happened all the time. If someone would introduce me or even when I was introducing myself, I would say, "Hi, I'm Annie, and I am on the tennis team!" It was like the only thing that really mattered about myself at that moment was what I did, accomplished, and was a part of. No one goes around introducing themselves saying, "Hi, I am _, and I have a big heart, love people, and am really good at forgiving!" Literally cringing at the thought of that right now, why? Because that is not what people do.

We define ourselves by what we do. It's been that way

for as long as I can remember. Even in kindergarten on the first day of school, they'd have us introducing ourselves, followed by the hobbies we liked to participate in. No one ever teaches us that there is a difference between what we do and who we are. It's almost as if the only things we are good for are the things that we do. I am here to remind you that you are, first and foremost, a child of God, and don't let anyone tell you differently. It doesn't matter what club you are in, what sport you play, what committee you are president of, or even the job status that you have; you are a child of God no matter what your status or lack thereof is at the moment. You can never lose that. Your worth is never lost because it is not in what you do that makes you worthy, but in Whose you are. You are His and His always. That is what makes you worthy, and that is what makes you *you*. You are not the different trophies you have in your closet, but the character you have in your heart. You are not the status of the corner parking spot in your office garage, but the kindness you show to the people who need it most. When God calls you, you don't have to answer with the list of things you *do*, but the one thing that you *are*, which is His.

God, I am yours. Always and forever. Help me release all of the things that I identify myself and worth by. You are the only thing that defines me.
Amen.

You've Never Failed Me Yet

> "And to know the love of Christ that surpasses knowledge, that you may be filled with all the fullness of God." Ephesians 3:19*

Right now, things are hard. The truth? They are hard for everyone. I think it is so easy to get consumed in the hardships of our own lives that we forget everyone has some type of "hard" going on for them at the moment. Everybody has been through things, everyone has had battles, and everyone will continue to go through hardships as long as they are on this earth.

In this particular moment for myself, I am so confused. We're all friends here, right? Well, let me just tell you, I used to think I had it all figured out. I had my five-year, heck, ten-year plan down to a science. It's funny how right when you get to the point where you feel like you have all things under control, all those little voices you ignored because they jeopardized your plan, start speaking a little bit louder.

It's like no matter how hard you try to ignore them because you know, by listening to them, it could mess up your whole plan; their volume increases simultaneously.

There have been a lot of little voices I haven't been paying attention to lately. Well, let me rephrase that- I have been giving them attention, just in the way that says, "I know you are there, but I am going to smush you down as far as you can go until I can pretend you aren't there anymore."

I'm really scared right now. I have no idea what I am doing, all I know is that I couldn't ignore the little voices in my head anymore, the ones that told me there is something more out there. There is more than just sitting back, settling down, and following my "plan." I feel this seed of greatness in my heart that I really want to follow, and the way I have been living my life the past couple of months isn't going to get me there. Sometime,s God puts experiences, people, and practices into your life to grow you to a certain point, but once you get to that point, you realize that to keep growing, you have to start giving up some of the habits that make you feel most comfortable. It isn't easy. One of the hardest things to do is give up what you feel the most comfortable with now for something in the future that you aren't even sure is going to happen. The truth is, though, God has never failed me yet, and He's never failed you yet, either. All those little voices have always led me to the right decision in the past, no matter how bad they hurt, and they will for you too. It's easy to want to ignore the things that you know in your gut are right for you, but I encourage you to start leaning into those voices in your head.

They are God's way of telling you that there is something more. He's never failed you yet, and how do I know that? Because you're here right now, reading this. The battles you've faced? You've gotten through them, and you ended up here, having this conversation with me in this book. He will always come and find you. He will always make a point to make sure you don't slip through the cracks. He will never leave you, and He will never cease going after you. He has never failed you yet and is not going to stop anytime soon.

God, here I am; scared, terrified, confused, tormented, upset, vulnerable, sinful, hurting, and all. Help me break and break open so that more of your light can fill me up.
Amen.

You Cannot Earn It

> *"Not that we are sufficient in ourselves to claim anything as coming from us, but our sufficiency is from God." 2 Corinthians 3:5*

It's so funny to me how I am constantly reminding other people of their finiteness, and how they can in no way, shape, or form earn God's love by any means, and yet when it comes to my own life, I very rarely walk the talk. It's like that saying, "common sense isn't always common practice." I know that I can't earn God's love or favor, but it's almost the very same second I am saying that out loud that I am also doing something to try and win His favor. Doesn't make sense, right? Take my writing career as a whole, for example. I never in a million years dreamed of being an author, and if we are being totally honest here- I still don't. I love to write, but not because I label myself as an "author," but because I feel called to write down the message God has put in my heart. If we are being honest here, it's also because this is way cheaper than therapy, and writing through all of the things I am feeling helps me release the tension that surrounds those feelings at the same time.

I have so many dreams. I have big dreams, smaller dreams, dreams that have kept me up at night for years, and dreams that came into my heart one day and out of my heart the next. I used to think that to fulfill the dreams God put in my heart, it required me to do everything perfectly. To not mess up. To consistently forge the path. To create my own opportunities. To create my own successes. In doing all of that, I now realize that I was preventing God from doing the one thing that He wants to do, which is to use His strength through me. If my dreams are to come true, it's going to be God making them possible, not me. You cannot earn it, my friends, because you already have it. Whatever that thing is you want so desperately that it literally keeps you from falling asleep at night, if it is in God's plan for you, you have already got it. There is nothing you can do to earn it. That is how good our God is, He *wants* to give us things. Now, do you have to put yourself in an open position to receive it? Absolutely. God cannot give you what you are closed off to receiving. However, release yourself of the fear that you have to be perfect to carry out God's purpose for your life. He gave you that purpose so that He could carry it out through you and show you how powerful He is.

God, here is my pressure. Take it all off of me. This was never about me being perfect, but about You having the grace to give me perfect love.
Amen.

Thank You for the Storms

> "He replied, 'You of little faith, why are you so
> afraid?' Then he got up and rebuked the winds and
> the waves, and it was completely calm."
> Matthew 8:26

I used to think that storms were God's way of showing He was mad at me. Isn't it funny what we used to think as kids? I remember being in the back of my mom's Toyota Sequoia after she had just picked me up from 6th grade, and it was pouring down rain. All I could think while I was sitting the backseat squished between my sister's panda bear roller backpack and the three bags of Chick Fil A, we had just picked up for lunch for the four of us was, "is God crying right now because I did something bad?" I genuinely used to think that the rain was God's tears.

As I have gotten older, my view on storms has changed a little bit. I'm not just talking about the kind I was looking at in that Toyota that particular day, but the ones on the inside. When you go through something traumatic, what no one ever talks about is how even though on the outside it looks like things are smoothed over, the storm on the inside continues to rage on. Even though you got out of the job, the way your boss treated you in that job still lingers and haunts you every single day. Despite the fact that the relationship that has been bringing you so much unrest is over, that feeling of not being good enough still plays like a broken record in your mind every time you try to get close to someone else. Although you may have moved away from that city with those people who abused you mentally, physically, or emotionally, the storm of their abuse still rages within your body despite your change in zip codes. I want to remind you that the storms we face make us stronger, they really do. God doesn't take away the storm, but He does provide us shelter within the storm if you look to Him. Storms don't really end, not at least in the way we hope them to. The things we have been through never truly go away, because just as physical pain leaves wounds that scar, so does emotional pain. However, please remember that those scars make you who you are. They shape you into the person God is using to bless this planet. God uses your pain for good. He uses your scars for blessings. He'll take your broken pieces and turn them into something beautiful. So, let the storms rage on. Instead of asking God for the storms to stop, just ask Him to give you refuge and be with you in them.

God, you take what the enemy means for evil, and you turn it for good. This storm will not have the last say. The storm isn't the end. The storm will lead to the scars that will tell my story and someday pave the way as the survival guide for someone else. Use me, all of me.
Amen.

Choose Your Hard

> *"So do not fear, for I am with you; do not be dismayed,*
> *for I am your God. I will strengthen you and help*
> *you; I will uphold you with my righteous right hand."*
> *Isaiah 41:10*

I am so tired of myself always trying to find a way to avoid the "hard." In workouts, I will spend an extra 15 minutes thinking of different exercises I could do to avoid doing the one exercise I absolutely loathe. In conversations, I will try to find a way to speak the one thing I really want to say but dread saying it because I know that will create conflict, and conflict is hard. When ice cream presents itself to me, I think of all the reasons I should absolutely eat the huge bowl of it and not feel bad because saying no is hard.

Guess what friends? No matter what we choose in life, there are going to be hardships. Speaking your mind is hard, but so is cowering in silence. Getting healthy is hard, but so is staying unhealthy. Following your dreams is hard, but so is not having the courage to follow your dreams. Leaving a relationship is hard, but so is trying to shrink back into a relationship you have outgrown. Trying new things is hard, but so is never challenging yourself to try anything at all.

God didn't put us here on this earth saying that things weren't going to be hard and that painful things weren't going to happen to us. He never promised that bad wouldn't happen. What He did promise us is that He would be there through us with it. So, I am asking you today, knowing that He is with you through all of the hard, what hard are you going to choose? Are you going to choose the easy path that leads to stagnation, complacency, and the pain of unexpressed potential? Or the hard path that leads to a continuous pursuit of the best version of yourself? It's always your choice. You get to choose your hard.

God, today I choose the hard that brings me closer to you. I choose the path that challenges me to become the best version of myself. The one that requires me to raise my hands and realize I cannot walk this path alone, but I don't have to because you promised to always be there with me.
Amen.

Faith in the Fire

> *"More than that, we rejoice in our sufferings, knowing that suffering produces endurance, and endurance produces character, and character produces hope, and hope does not put us to shame, because God's love has been poured into our hearts through the Holy Spirit who has been given to us." Romans 5:3-5*

God never promised us that nothing bad was going to happen to us. This is something that has taken me so long to understand, and even now, I have moments where I wonder why in the world God would allow something like this to happen to me if He loves me so much. The thing is, God never promised us a life without struggle. I think that's what the promise of Heaven is for. Now, this is just my own thinking, but I look at life almost as if it is the big warm-up for everything that is to come with God's promises. God is so good, and Heaven is going to be so good, but life right now isn't always good. I think that's the point, though, to see if we still raise our hands and sing hallelujah even when we are walking in storms. Even when we are walking in the fire, and it burns, are we still looking up at our God and saying that we know He is the God of the hills and the valleys? Do we keep our faith even when it gets hard?

Life isn't supposed to be easy. It isn't supposed to only be filled with good things. That is what Heaven is for. This world still has incredible things in it if you look for them, but I do acknowledge that not every day is going to be roses and rainbows. You know what, though? Every single battle you are facing right now is molding you into the person God is shaping you to be. The good, the bad, the ugly, the pretty, and the not so pretty; all life's moments are a chance to continue to raise your hands toward Him, even when you question and even when it's hard. I just had a conversation with God that ended very much like, "if you're even there, can you just remind me of your goodness," because honestly, at that moment, I felt so alone and doubtful. Hear me when I say that doubt is not the absence of faith, but the means to have it. Doubt gives you the space you need to have faith. This is what allows you to have faith in the fire, knowing that even in your most doubtful moments, His goodness doesn't slow down, stall, or cease.

God, no matter how much I push away, fall short, or go through, you are always still there. You are the only true constant in my life. Give me the strength to continue to face you, embrace you, and raise my hands to you even in the midst of the battle. You are my armor, my protector, and my refuge.
Amen.

You Cannot Mess It Up

Maybe you're like me, a ruminator, as my personality assessment likes to call it. I could ruminate on all the possible scenarios of every single situation for literally the rest of my life, I think. I could also place a highly confident bet that I have spent most of my life already ruminating on every decision, big or small, I have made up to this point as a 22-year-old. Recently, I made an incredibly hard decision to let someone go out of my life, and I will be so honest, you guys, I wasn't 100% sure. Every scenario went through my head of the "what-ifs," the "could-be's," the "maybe's." The thing is, we all kill ourselves every single day on the "what-if's" of life. We wrack our brains over every possible fact or figure that represents why one choice is better than the other, outweighing all the pro's and con's, and still reach the same conclusion that is we aren't entirely sure.

I used to be so scared of making decisions because I was afraid I'd mess up God's plans for me. I so badly wanted to do the right thing by God, and make sure that whatever I chose aligned with what He would've chosen for me, and recently, I realized how absolutely insane that is. If you are anything like me, you need to hear this. You cannot mess up the plans God has for your life. How do I know this? Because He turns graces into gardens, ashes into beauty, seas into highways, and dead people into resurrected people. He also turns your mistakes into your good. He blesses all your pain, suffering, wrong decisions, poor choices, and misguided steps into a beautiful brand-new creation that furthers your relationship with Him and your faith in what He can do with your life.

What freedom would you let yourself feel if you knew that you couldn't make the wrong choice? No matter what, you will still have His love, and that is the greatest victory. Stop wracking your head around all of the possible ways you can go wrong and start realizing the only way you can go right has already be chosen for you. God's love is there for you, whether you make the "right" decision or not. Free yourself from the burden of carrying a responsibility for always making the right choices that you were never asked to carry.

God, I have your love. I can't go wrong when I have that. You love me unconditionally, and that in itself is all I need to know to live out the life I feel freed to live. Amen.

100 Days Later,

And you have made it! 100 days of being reminded of the beautiful, one of a kind, exquisite, magnificent light that is YOU.

Now that we know each other a little better, or at least you know all of my deepest fears, thoughts, anxieties, insecurities, and personal reflections, I feel as if I have a place to tell you this with some authority. The world needs you. Yes, I am talking to *you*.

Do you realize that there is literally no one else like you on this earth? The way your hair is curly or straight, the freckles on your nose or lack thereof, the dimple beneath your nose, the sparkle in your eye, the way you squinch your nose or purse your lips, how you walk, talk, think, move, act, behave, laugh, snort, giggle, and crack jokes; every single thing about you makes you the person you are. I know, for a fact, you still have something left to do on this earth, because if you didn't, you physically wouldn't be here to read these words on this page. If you're not dead, you're not done on this earth. There is some purpose God needs you to fulfill in this world that only you can do. You are special, my friend. You are worthy. You are *capable*. Did you know that? I mean, did you *really* know that.

I think it is one thing to know it, but another thing to live it. What if every single day you decided to live the truth that there is actually no one else on this earth made like you? How would you carry yourself?

You have a light inside you that is begging to be shown. I once read that the light inside our souls can only be shown after we break open a little. Stop trying to be perfect and prevent yourself from falling. It is in our falls, failures, and breaking points that we create an opportunity to be broken open, so God's light that He put inside of us can shine through even more. You have a gift inside your heart that this world is craving, my dear, don't you dare try to cover it up.

Live into your gifts. Expose your inner beauty. Shine your love.

Be the light.
Xoxo, *Annie*

Made in the USA
Columbia, SC
05 April 2024

34032002R00136